THE TERTIARY I

What Road to Inclusive High

Edited by Chris Duke

niace
promoting adult learning

Published by the National Institute of Adult Continuing Education (England and Wales)

21 De Montfort Street
Leicester LE1 7GE
Company registration no. 2603322
Charity registration no. 1002775

promoting adult learning

NIACE has a broad remit to promote lifelong learning opportunities for adults. NIACE works to develop increased participation in education and training, particularly for those who do not have easy access because of class, gender, age, race, language and culture, learning difficulties or disabilities, or insufficient financial resources.

You can find NIACE online at www.niace.org.ul

Cataloguing in Publication Data
A CIP record of this title is available from the British Library

ISBN 1 86201 235 0

Typeset by Kerrypress Ltd, Luton
Printed by Latimer Trend, Plymouth

Contents

Contributors

Professor Robert Burgess Vice-Chancellor, University of Leicester

Dr Philip Candy Director, The NHSU Institute, National Health Service University

Kath Dentith Assistant Director Access, Quality Assurance Agency for Higher Education

Professor Chris Duke Associate Director Higher Education, NIACE and RMIT University

Professor Neil Garrod Deputy Vice-Chancellor, Thames Valley University

Laurence Howells Director of Learning Policy and Strategy, Scottish Funding Council

Professor Geoff Layer Pro-Vice-Chancellor, University of Bradford, and Director, Action on Access

Professor Sir Howard Newby Chief Executive, Higher Education Funding Council for England

Professor Gareth Parry University of Sheffield

Adrian Perry Senior Visiting Fellow, University of Sheffield

Professor Richard Taylor Director, Institute of Continuing Education, University of Cambridge

Professor David Vincent Pro-Vice-Chancellor, Open University

Professor Sir David Watson Vice-Chancellor, University of Brighton

Kevin Whitston Higher Education Funding Council for England

Foreword

It is a considerable pleasure to introduce this NIACE publication on 'the tertiary moment'. This volume presents a valuable opportunity to develop the debate on post-compulsory education.

The contribution of higher and further education to the knowledge economy now and in the future should not be under-estimated. All learning is valuable, whether it is training individuals directly for work, preparing them for the challenges of tomorrow, or education for its own sake which contributes to a wider culture of learning and community engagement. A central feature will be developing our understanding of boundaries between the 'academic' and the 'vocational'. These barriers have never been static and are becoming increasingly permeable. The education sectors and students themselves are not well served by continuing arguments about whether engineering, medicine or media studies are academic or vocational subjects. The vital conversation to be had is how higher education can engage with the skills agenda and how we create new opportunities for a wider range of learners.

Together we need to address the present inequalities, to enable a more diverse range of students to access the full range of educational opportunities. The pathways from GCSE and A levels are well recognised, but those students undertaking 'vocationally orientated' qualifications at levels 2 and 3 rarely have a clear view of the opportunities that should be open to them. There is a need to contest the conventional view of the non-A-level student, and to reflect this in the growth of new and existing courses, curricula and assessment procedures.

The challenge of a higher education system fit for twenty-first-century purposes is to address these challenges while remaining robust in our pursuit of high quality education and research. In thinking about how we might develop post-compulsory education, innovative ways of institutional connectivity are needed to give learners the opportunities to cross educational boundaries and to fulfil their potential.

The following papers set out some of the key issues that will shape the future landscape. Contributions discuss the divide between vocational and academic learning, the tensions between collaboration and market forces, and the inter-relationship of our funding and policy mechanisms. This volume represents a welcome addition to the debate, and a tribute to the higher education sector's ongoing commitment to widening participation.

Sir Howard Newby
Chief Executive, Higher Education Funding Council for England

CHAPTER ONE

The crab's progress:[1] Approaching a tertiary system for lifelong learning

Chris Duke

Preamble

In June 2004 the NIACE Policy Committee debated a paper, 'Towards an inclusive tertiary system for lifelong learning', and resolved in favour of a seminar to consider the subject further.[2] One issue that arose was simply 'What is the higher education and lifelong learning debate really about?' What do we need of the higher education system and are lacking that is obscured in the many words and initiatives? And for NIACE as the adult learners' organisation, how to advance the needs of adult learners without embracing the whole system and policy agenda, if not the whole *problematique* of modern globalised society?

Another question was why and how far to stretch the notion of 'university' to encompass all new uses and forms including the corporate, electronic or virtual, and the for-profit. Should we cease fighting to protect the words 'university' and 'higher' and let quality, reputation and the market take care of this? Should we seek again to define what is essentially *higher* about higher education; or concentrate, rather, on the notion of 'lifelong', enhancing access and approaching universal participation in society's cultural-intellectual goods? This would mean clarifying which cultural, technical and social skills are needed and can be used by all citizens of all ages and for all purposes.

How far can higher education and the university be opened out through work-based learning, and integrated across other sectors and portfolios? Can universities retain a quasi-monopolistic role if learning is lifelong and life-wide? How can wider access to the resources of higher education for both initial and post-experience adult learners avoid 'dumbing-down'? Is the whole venture doomed by the job-allocating function of higher education? Can we accept that a distinctively class-conscious and snobbish society, yet one suspicious of privilege, differential status and prestige, will always mean unequal market opportunities and keen competition for entry to elite institutions? Can one work constructively and realistically with this grain without abandoning hope for a more healthy and sustainable society?

This chapter sets out issues canvassed in the seminar on 16 November 2004, and then draws out some threads from the day's discussion. The succeeding chapters were revised from papers presented on that occasion, or contributed subsequently by others involved in that event.

Where to start?

One may begin with the desirable or the actual. What is needed of an emergent system of universal higher or tertiary education? The OECD term *tertiary*, described by one author as helpfully provocative, may encourage fresh thinking.

The 'client' of higher education now needs to be the whole of society. In the twentieth century it was the individual learner, typically – and in the policy-making mind – one moving on from secondary into higher education. The late twentieth-century debate was about student numbers, system size, cost and cost-sharing, about labour market needs and the shape of an affordable system to handle rapid growth.

In practice *the whole society as client* is coming to mean in significant part the local or regional 'community', its economic and social health as well as its age participation rate (APR) and wider compass of participation. Measures and indicators then reach out into health and welfare, sustainability including the environment, economic growth and innovation. Universities and colleges will be judged across indicators more ambitious and revealing than today's aggregation of research output and individual study attainment.

As this is worked through, regional 'place-based' measures will join other indicators of the performance of higher education. An *engaged* university contributing to sustainable socio-economic well-being will be judged by reference to the *knowledge or learning society*. The adult learner will be as fully habilitated as the young first-time student, neither more nor less valued and thought important.

What has been achieved so far, and what serious issues remain?

The year 2004 was dominated by debate about higher and differential fees, and about mechanisms to prod and steer the system in directions chosen by Government. Preoccupation with fees, and with the Office for Fair Access (OFFA) agenda – fair queuing to enter high-prestige institutions – diverted attention from such other matters as wider participation and the circumstances of part-time students.

Adult access and participation are largely equated with part-time study. Despite intensive and influential lobbying we entered 2005 still burdened by the unhelpful separation between full- and part-time modes of funding higher education and managing learning. The unintended consequences, not just for Birkbeck, the Open University and their students but system-wide, remained to be discovered.

Inequality of access by social class is on the agenda across all parties, notwithstanding differences about system size, function and funding. Yet progress in reducing inequality remains modest, although significant funds and attention now go to widening participation among the young. Like *lifelong learning*, widening participation is acknowledged in almost any policy statement to do with higher education.

Differentiation within the sector is getting sharper, but not in useful and complementary ways. A hard-won place in a new, 'mainly teaching', university may be devalued by competitive abuse, one-dimensional league tables, and talk of plunging standards. Is it a prize not worth winning? This presents a problem for all parties and partners. Solving it deserves the attention of institutions across the whole Universities United Kingdom (UUK) spectrum, if only for reasons of self-interest.

Higher within further education remains problematic. This is now the Learning and Skills Council (LSC) rather than further education sector. The regionalised LSC is all but exclusively focused on level 2 and level 3 attainment, deflecting its attention from higher education within further education. The 'mixed economy colleges' (MECs) have a difficult predicament, less shared now by the colleges of higher education which see the light of university status down the tunnel.

Support for students remains unequal between further and higher education. Yet upper- and post-secondary-level vocational education enjoys high priority. Foundation Degrees sit centre stage in matters to do with access, progression, economic development and the vocational curriculum agenda. But this remains an unsatisfactory and inherently contradictory policy arena, plagued by problems of identity, credibility and support. Without effectively joined-up tertiary thinking, and preferably a common policy-making and funding methodology, progress continues only crabwise.

On the other hand many higher education institutions, especially in the Colleges and New Universities sectors, brilliantly enable wider adult access and participation. They devise new modes for raising aspiration, attract first-generation and other non-traditional students, older as well as young, and provide support relevant to needs. Premium funding helps a little, but the cost of retaining and supporting the successful completion of a wide spectrum of students remains burdensome.

As such institutions acquire more distinctive access missions at the expense of a conventional (Mode One) research identity we may need to worry even more about inequity, failures of progression and the poor functioning of credit transfer. System diversity remains an unsolved puzzle, if not a looming disaster, both in terms of individual aspiration and disappointment and in terms of the whole sector engaging with innovation and development across the several fields of scholarship, and being valued for all of it.

If this is problematic, so too is the current framing of policy, which is formulated in supply(-side)–demand(-side) terms. Demand may be by individuals, employers or perhaps 'the economy'. The market, and autonomous institutions, are in principle not to be interfered with. Demand, however, is often not for what government (and in principle therefore society) needs. The 'client' of higher education should be the whole society. Supply–demand dualism must therefore extend to the triangle of need–demand–supply. Until then policy-making will be self-deluding.[3]

Immediate and medium-term prospects

What might reasonably be sought over the next two to five years?

It would correspond with the reality of participation and move us more confidently in a direction made necessary by the new demography to put adults firmly within the mental set of higher education policy-making.

Achieving such a change – of focus, perception, language and paradigm – means fully accepting the *new demography*. The change is becoming inescapable in the work and pensions arenas of economically advanced societies, but the impact on tertiary and higher education is barely acknowledged. The short life-cycle of technology has yet to be translated into labour market terms. Along with a modernised understanding of 'career planning' and counselling goes a proper grasp of *lifelong learning for longer life working*.

More tangibly, the backwash of the higher education White Paper, and the close-run legislation that followed, present opportunities to improve support for adult part-time students based on mode-free, module-based funding according to study load, with cross-party backing and informal governmental support. The more older adults are written back into the equity agenda alongside the younger target clientele of Aimhigher and school partnerships, the better the chance of using some top-up fee income for needy adult students, irrespective of their age and mode of study.

A more holistic approach to the equity and wider participation agenda may also be possible if different influence groups can work together on unfinished business from the White Paper (DfES 2003). Widely shared social values might come together with the economic and demographic agenda. The November 2004 Seminar however demonstrated how hard it can be to translate values shared at a high level of generality into policy and strategy for a particular moment and place.

What else is possible – what are the main obstacles?

It may help to distinguish between a natural time-lag in innovation and deeper cultural resistances tapped into by resistant interest groups. Problems may have more to do with failure to implement change determined as policy than with lack of vision. A high level of consensus on such matters does not of itself make them happen.

Powerful interests benefit from present arrangements and see little merit in changes favouring an older clientele, more vocationalism, or less inequality. The University of Bristol knows about this, but is perhaps with determination finding a way through it.[4] Public, media, political and administrator attitudes and stereotypes can be problematic: parts of the press, sometimes the schools, a Cabinet familiar with just one kind of higher education.

The institutions and their academic staff may entrench interests, the effect of which is conservative. Academic autonomy faces off government in regional planning; many academic staff embrace disciplines and resist deep curriculum change – not without merit, since universities must conserve as well as invent.

The rising inequality of recent decades may normalise and legitimate inequality: is it again OK and healthy to be, and to be seen to be celebrating being, seriously rich? Has God again ordered the estate of the rich man and the poor man, in England as globally?

Another difficulty arises from persisting policy and administrative segmentation. 'Joined-up-ness' is honoured in the breach; silos reproduce themselves. We lack a legitimated higher and tertiary education planning body. The Higher Education Funding Council for England (HEFCE) is emphatically a non-planning body,[5] and even HEFCE has difficulty joining up its own several strategic priority areas. Being everywhere yet nowhere, lifelong learning disappears down the cracks. Adult learners are in practice marginalised as funding follows the 18–30 agenda. We talk the needs of students but honour the convenience of structures.

Finally, a target and audit culture denies trust and undermines confidence. Addiction to audit and risk assessment defers ultimately inevitable larger changes. And yet, paradoxically, the sector is destabilised by administrative impatience and what seems almost a mania for interfering short-cycle innovation. Return-on-investment-driven reductionism may discourage increasingly short-serving institutional heads from undertaking anything long-term.

What are the big issues for NIACE? NIACE is principally concerned with adult learning opportunities, but the context of global competition and destabilisation cannot sensibly be ignored. We inhabit a world of OECD indicators and comparative competition; *Education at a Glance* (OECD 2004) for example highlights return on investment. Globally relevant and locally important is the ageing and otherwise changing demography. The wider agenda goes beyond the vocational, into civic, environmental, and social inclusion arenas.

Managing extreme complexity and successive insoluble puzzles is taking us towards greater regional devolution. This may be to create more manageable size.[6] It affects tertiary and higher education, creating a new context for institutional autonomy within a planning region. It suggests a broader curriculum, looking past today's occupation and employment sector to an unknowable labour market beyond.

The new fascination with *engagement* may disturb much that has been assumed and protected, bringing together individuals, 'community' and place on an altered tertiary landscape.[7]

Lifelong learning networks – how promising a way forward?

Can lifelong learning networks be made to work for lifelong learning?

An addition to the furniture of tertiary education is the lifelong learning network (LLN). It would be gullible to think that LLNs are popular or welcome in a widening participation community where uncertainty and rapid change, new rules and requirements invite cynicism. On the other hand, the high profile of currently better-resourced widening participation, with the possibility of more new resources to follow, should new funded student numbers flow through the networks, has helped prepare the way.

The job description of the LLN falls short of the name, and short of what the optimistic hope that it might become. It may however come to look less like the latest ephemeral idea among new configurations from a ministerial office than a permanent feature of the changing local–regional landscape. On the surface it is to raise the progression and retention rates of 14+ youngsters on vocational routes into higher education, reducing the 90 per cent : 50 per cent differential in take-up between academic and vocational pathways.

Why should NIACE care about the networks?

This would be an important thing to achieve. It might add support and critical mass to Foundation Degrees, which remain on trial. It might help to address social class inequality. Yet it might still appear of only marginal interest to NIACE.

Formative thinking and early indications of a field response suggest otherwise. The vocational agenda applies no less to adults than to school and further education college leavers. LLNs insist on Sector Skills Councils and Centres of Vocational Excellence involvement. These might at the least support accredited and better integrated workplace and work-based learning, breathing new life into a faltering credit recognition and transfer agenda and making it work at local and regional level.

More ambitiously the networks, which will begin locking into place in 2006 after a piloting and building period, could become one basis for a new *recurrency* in tertiary and higher education. As an abiding institutional form built on an acceptable *modus vivendi* with network members whose free-standing identity they initially appear to compromise, they might come to give regional and lifelong tertiary provision new force and substance.

This would take us beyond *alternation* in the original OECD *recurrent education for lifelong learning* thesis[8] to a practical idea of *lifelong learning membership*. Locality based, this idea is potentially stronger and wider than *alumni*, largely equated with fund-raising. The 'contract' to study for a diploma or degree might become a lifelong service agreement, especially valued in a context of regional development but transferable in respect of labour mobility.

For adult learners this would transcend the dichotomy between initial (18+ or deferred) tertiary education and continuing education or continuing professional development. Continuing connectedness with the multiple and complementary resources of a network might begin to ameliorate elite hierarchy. Recurrent participation and progression can be in multiple directions through life.[9] This would end the silliness of becoming the for-life 'master' of a subject, a title which suggests that the need to learn is over. It might even open up a discussion of drop-out and wastage so as to value not only completed degrees but also cumulative and partial 'completion'.

Maybe lifelong learning networks can open the way to fully engaged open-system tertiary provision where the adult is a normal student – a repeat-business paying customer.

If the networks can bring widening participation and 'third stream' community engagement strategies together this might also enable mutually beneficial and complementary partnership, inching us crabwise towards an elusive win-win solution to the dilemma of diversity.

There are many 'mights', a lot of conditionality, in all of this. Much devil resides in the detail of how networks are negotiated, formed and initially developed. Looking across the broader tertiary agenda in summary form, a modest programme of action might look like this:

- Press for mode-free funding of more integrated part- and full-time study options;
- Continue to campaign for 'the new demography';
- Value and finance further education, including higher education within further education, as essential to an integrated tertiary system;
- Create strong premiums, reward systems, and sanctions to support progression, including full recognition and portability of credit;
- Consider introducing (a) annual mature student audits and (b) mature study impact statements at institutional level;
- Make lifelong learning networks work as new institutions for lifelong learning;
- Replace *drop-out* and *wastage* with *partial completion* and *progression* in the policy lexicon;
- Request a little less impatience over its initiatives on the part of government.

The Tertiary Seminar – themes and issues

In the words of David Vincent (see Chapter 9) 'the turning point was Howard Newby's Colin Bell Memorial Lecture' in March 2004.[10] And in Howard Newby's words writing about the Research Assessment Exercise a little later, 'the dilemmas we face are not unique to the UK, but the English genius for converting diversity into hierarchy has distorted the debate here'.[11] A crude over-simplification of the Bradford conference at which the Colin Bell

Memorial Lecture was delivered might be that in the United States it is all about race, in England about class.

The chapters that follow were written by the authors as individual scholars and practitioners to contribute to a 'Chatham House' discussion of the configuration of higher education and the prospects for lifelong learning networks from an adult learner perspective. The papers by Dentith, Parry, Perry and Whitston were written following the discussion. Candy was unable to take part but his paper was available to the seminar.

NIACE opened its own public engagement with the notion of *tertiary* in a conference in London a year earlier – see *Adults Learning* 15.7 (March 2004) for a sense of that discussion (NIACE 2004). Lifelong learning networks (LLNs) were coming over the horizon by the time the papers in this book were invited. It, like the Seminar, set out to connect the broader issue of system shape and purpose – 'thinking tertiary' – with more specific issues that arise as lifelong learning networks move from the formative towards the operational. The sequence of the following chapters roughly reflects this duality.

The question whether and if so why England is different threads through the discussion, the differences within the UK sharpened with devolution and echoed in the perspective offered by Laurence Howells from the newly integrated Scottish Funding Council. Despite proximity to continental Europe the easiest analogies for the planning and funding of higher education, including widening participation, tend to be with the 'old Commonwealth', while the reference point and model favoured politically is usually that of the United States with its stronger private sector, alumni and benefactor traditions and developments. The Californian and Wisconsin systems have attracted favourable attention as proposed models for open progression through a layered system. The emergent networks have been characterised as prospective mini-Wisconsins.[12]

Tertiary is a thought-provocative term in English higher education. We may distinguish between 'thinking and planning tertiary' and creating a unified tertiary funding system. New Zealand has recently grasped the concept fully, in creating a unitary Tertiary Education Commission for the whole of post-school including community adult education. Australia earlier dismantled its Commonwealth Tertiary Education Commission, with the merging of the colleges of advanced education into a single higher education sector. The separate funding of technical and further education (TAFE) makes for great difficulty in the dual-sector (TAFE and higher education) universities in Victoria. In this volume Neil Garrod examines the start-up of England's first major dual-sector university. We will see how it manages the distinct funding streams and methodologies – predictably with difficulty. On the other hand it will be important to see how far a unitary institutional administration is able to facilitate progression within rather than between institutions.

In Scotland real change in funding is taking place. The term tertiary was put to work to bring further and higher education closer together. Abandoned at the last fence, the term can be said to have been effective – a war won with integrative funding, while the term was let drop. The next step will be as John

Field suggests in *Adults Learning* 16.3, published in November 2004 just as this Seminar was conducted: after hyperbolic end-of-civilised-life furore greeting the Scottish tertiary funding, the real work of creating well-used pathways, articulation, progression and further development remains to be done. The compromise to abandon the term tertiary and the provocative *STEPS* – 'specified tertiary education providers' – in the face of wails 'heard from Edinburgh to Aberdeen', cost little. The question this suggests is how far the English Higher Education Funding Council (HEFCE), and behind it the government, will be willing to give teeth – and money – to the new networks to do their job. If OFFA (the Office for Fair Access) could have its teeth so easily drawn, what are the prospects for networks? Is there a different cultural base, and stronger democratic instinct underpinning educational opportunity, north of the border?

What was the general flavour of the animated discussion through the Seminar? Optimism battled scepticism and some quite bleak pessimism – the glass half-full or half-empty. A familiar theme was not conservatism so much as initiative-weariness, and weariness at the burden of distrustful interfering, auditing, and bureaucratic duplication. Apropos networks there surfaced a quite intransigent dichotomy – between local arrangements and progression, and national and wider mobility for all in the age of Bologna. The subversion of generous intent (exemplified by OFFA) attracted scathing comment, with reference to snobbishness as well as endemic hierarchy.

Networks, it was concluded, must be given a go, but there is concern about mixed messages and the plurality of models, some based on place, others on specialisms. Regionalism and the role of RDAs (regional development agents) lurked in the wings, with a sense that planning that belonged centrally was being sloughed off to a yet less acceptable regional level. The issue of institutional autonomy does not thereby go away, or get easier to resolve.

There was – not always sympathetic – concern that HEFCE might be wriggling under irreconcilable tensions, and perhaps less clear acknowledgement that as ever we are faced with a sub-optimal balance between ideal and pragmatic. How far will the more prestigious universities be confronted as to their regional and widening participation obligations in the face of world-class research imperatives? Do networks present a way for them of resolving this problem? Can the networks become truly comprehensive, such that every citizen falls within their benevolent cover of opportunity? If so, this presumably makes geography the dominant axis in any matrix, to be addressed for remote communities by good distance learning tools and supports.

Another important theme and tension had to do with building on what we have, versus creating anew. The keenest source of likely resentment and resistance is proving to be a sense that existing arrangements and past efforts are now to be pushed aside in favour of a new idea. On the other hand, the compromises, rivalries and irrationalities of today should not be carried through into an ambitious new design for tomorrow. The more subtle tension behind this is that the funding council is resented for any attempt to steer and shape the system to a general, let along a grand, plan. Yet it comes under criticism for approaching networks in an unusually open, exploratory and iterative way, not laying down precisely what shape and size networks should be but indicating rather than tightly prescribing purposes, and seeking to build through self-nominating non-competing consortia that are then funded to work up their ideas.

Was it perhaps characteristically English that participants were in the main more able to critique proposals before them than to suggest a vision for a system, with or without networks, to widen participation and extend lifelong and life-wide learning? We are perhaps better at mourning what we have lost and defending what we have than at visualising what might be.

Meanwhile HEFCE is evidently open to advice, feedback and shared learning about how to make the networks a worthwhile development. It combines the idea of letting many flowers bloom with a need to set threshold conditions, to provide a planning frame from the top in which different local and indigenous models can grow up. Feedback from this discussion suggested that thinking was grandiose, and yet too limited in the formal brief for networks; and that if unintended consequences for what already exists and for existing good relations rings alarm bells these should be heeded.

Succeeding chapters consider many issues and dimensions not mentioned in this introduction. David Vincent held that the whole higher education system needed to reverse out of the widening participation cul-de-sac in which it found itself. There was discussion as to how networks could really be learner-centred and empower learners when administrative requirements and categories ruled. We should think about what contributes to lifelong learning rather than what lifelong learning is, according to Howells – one system, many learners. David Watson compared different planning and managing timescales with the reproduction rates of the fruit-fly and the turtle.

For NIACE in this age of what Richard Taylor called *marketised welfarism*, there is another tension: between tending the Institute's own corner of adult learning opportunities within higher education, and engaging in the bigger debates about the purposes, shape and character of the whole higher education system. Without the latter, the former can make little mark. Moreover, adult learning within higher education (which can of course be equated with all higher education when one is adult by 18) is a subset of adult learning opportunities at all levels.

Just to say this reminds of greater inequalities. It suggests something more like the New Zealand approach – in a much smaller society – to tertiary comprehensiveness, as 'universal higher education' continues its march, driven by economic, technological and demographic change. Perhaps the networks will draw us crabwise in this direction. No less ambitiously, perhaps their Achilles' heel of focused vocationalism can be turned to advantage and allow reclamation of *vocational* and *vocation* in discourse and behaviour.

Notes

1   Crabs are renowned for scuttling rapidly sideways when alarmed. Soldier crabs also have a habit of retreating rapidly down holes and pulling a lid over their heads when danger threatens.
2   An earlier version of this paper, prepared in the context of the 2003 Higher Education White Paper (DfES 2003), may be found on the NIACE website.
3   How to protect scarce subjects exemplifies this problem.
4   See the paper presented by Barry Taylor to the August 2004 OECD Seminar on media and higher education (Taylor 2004).
5   And yet, as Mary Stuart states in debating this subject, 'for the learners' sakes, some form of planning is essential'. See the symposium, 'Thinking and planning tertiary', in the NIACE journal *Adults Learning* 15.7 (March 2004).
6   More cynically it pushes the blame for failure down the line and away from elected central government.
7   See in particular the work of Michael Gibbons through the Association of Commonwealth Universities including the 2003 ACU publication co-edited by Svava Bjarnason and Patrick Coldstream (Bjarnason and Coldstream 2003).
8   See the defining OECD CERI publication *Recurrent Education: Towards a Strategy for Lifelong Learning* (OECD CERI 1973).
9   It is a decade since Australia discovered to its surprise that progression from university to technical and further education (TAFE), the equivalent of further education in the UK, far outstripped progression from TAFE into HE.
10 Published in Geoff Layer (ed.), *Closing the Equity Gap: Impact of Widening Participation Strategies in the UK and USA* NIACE, 2005.
11 *Education Guardian*, 23 November 2004, p. 7.
12 See also, however, the recent study of progression systems and options, especially the way that the California and British Columbia systems work (Bekhradnia 2004).

References

Bekhradnia, Bahram (2004) *Credit Accumulation and Transfer, and the Bologna Process: An Overview*. Oxford: HEPI.

Bjarnason, Svava, and Patrick Coldstream (eds) (2003) *The Idea of Engagement: Universities in Society*. London: ACU.

DfES (Department for Education and Skills) (2003) *The Future of Higher Education*. London: The Stationery Office.

Field, John (2004) 'More needed for coherent system', *Adults Learning* 16.3.

Layer, Geoff (ed.) (2005) *Closing the Equity Gap: Impact of Widening Participation Strategies in the UK and USA*. Leicester: NIACE.

NIACE (2004) 'Thinking and planning tertiary', *Adults Learning* 15.7.

OECD (2004) *Education at a Glance.* Paris: OECD.

OECD CERI (1973) *Recurrent Education: Towards a Strategy for Lifelong Learning.* Paris: OECD.

Stuart, Mary (2004) 'Not made here', *Adults Learning* 15.7.

Taylor, Barry (2004) 'The risks associated with repositioning a university in the higher education market: how the University of Bristol found itself at the eye of a storm, and how it managed the crisis' (paper to OECD IMHE Seminar on Communicating Higher Education: Image and Reality, August 2004). Bristol: University of Bristol.

Although they have been revised for publication, the views expressed in this book remain those of the authors in their personal capacities, and are not to be attributed to their respective organisations. Likewise, they do not necessarily represent the views of NIACE.

Purposes and settings

CHAPTER TWO

Promoting lifelong learning networks: some unexpected allies

Philip C. Candy

Preamble

For as long as I have been professionally involved in the field of education – some three decades now – an integrated system of lifelong learning has been the goal of enlightened policy-makers, administrators and practitioners (not to mention learners) everywhere. And yet, in some ways, the goal seems as elusive now as it did back in 1972 when Edgar Faure and the Unesco Commission on the Future of Education first introduced the term 'lifelong learning' into the general educational lexicon (Faure 1972). Like a mirage shimmering on the horizon, it always seems both tantalisingly close and unreachably distant.

There are plenty of barriers to its realisation. One is the lack of precise agreement about what it means; despite (or perhaps because of) a voluminous literature there is a multiplicity of different interpretations of the term and of what it would look like in practice. A second obstacle is the inertia of the past – not only old systems, structures and funding models, but also old habits and thought patterns, which insist on seeing education as divided into non-overlapping domains both chronologically and administratively. A third category of obstacles is the earnest but sometimes overly complex arguments made on the basis of subtle – even casuistic – distinctions between different kinds of knowledge. Fourth, there are historical and conceptual challenges. In particular where would we draw the line between formal education on the one hand, and libraries, museums, health services and environmental agencies – indeed the myriad different organisations which collectively provide the context for learning in our society – on the other? Finally, there are practical stumbling-blocks too: political, organisational and financial impediments such as who would pay for a system of lifelong learning; how would schools, colleges and universities be organised differently; and which ministries or departments would take responsibility for providing coordinated learning opportunities for all citizens?

While there are powerful – if frequently invisible – forces ranged against the realisation of a system of lifelong learning (and beyond that, the ideal of the learning society), there are also compelling arguments in its favour. Although many of these are aspirational and ideological in tone and tenor, it is my contention that there are at least three specific phenomena that might hold out the potential for realising this goal. They are:

- the recent rate of change, and the consequences this has for views of knowledge (notably recognising the importance of tacit knowledge);
- the vital but often overlooked capacity of learners themselves to make a personally meaningful and satisfying tapestry from their learning experiences; and
- the increasing ubiquity of technology platforms that are blurring formerly rigid distinctions.

In the balance of this chapter I discuss how these three factors might advance the cause of lifelong learning, providing a more fertile context than hitherto for the success of the recently announced lifelong learning networks.

The pace of change as an ally

It has become increasingly commonplace – almost *de rigeur* – to complain about the pace of change – social, cultural, technological, economic, environmental, political and so on – in our society. Concepts such as 'blur', 'the weightless economy', 'business at the speed of thought', 'knowledge explosion', 'data smog', and 'information overload' all seek to capture and convey the unrelenting and unconstrained nature of this change. It is often implied, if not directly stated, that this change is difficult to deal with and, except for a few individuals and organisations that stand to gain from it, largely unwelcome.

While there can be little doubt that frequent and widespread change is challenging many enduring verities and basic assumptions, and that it is somewhat unsettling as a result, there is likewise little doubt that continuous change can be an ally in making the case for lifelong learning, because it unambiguously emphasises the need for continuing learning.

Perhaps more importantly, though, rapid and pervasive change calls into question some otherwise unproblematic assumptions about the enduring and invariant nature of knowledge. If one assumes that knowledge is fixed and stable, there may be grounds for arguing that it naturally resides in a particular domain – in higher education, or further education, or practice, or in the realm of intuition – and there may therefore be some basis for resisting the demand for lifelong learning approaches. But if new information is constantly coming to light, and ubiquitous change is creating the need for continuous adaptation, then surely the basis for resisting lifelong learning because knowledge is held to be immutable is also brought into question.

In other words, the ubiquity of change is altering the epistemological assumptions on which much of our current approach to education and training is based. Consequently we are experiencing a fundamental shift in much of the knowledge upon which existing understandings of learning – especially formal learning – have traditionally been based.

Learners as makers of meaning

If assumptions about the nature of knowledge are being turned upside-down, so too are assumptions about the nature of learning. Much of our formal system of education and training has traditionally been based on a transmission model of learning, where it is assumed that information is somehow conveyed intact and without distortion from the teacher to the learner. This assumption tacitly undergirds the persistence of most existing education systems and structures, including the division of the learning journey into discrete 'slices'. As a result it militates against the development of a lifelong learning approach whereby learners would be enabled to move seamlessly between and among various education providers.

However, an alternative (and increasingly widely accepted) view maintains that it is the learners themselves who provide the 'glue' that holds together their understandings. Rather than being passive recipients of information and insights purveyed by others, learners are active makers of meaning.

This so-called constructivist view puts the responsibility for learning where it rightly belongs: with the learner. It also provides a solid psychological background for the whole enterprise of lifelong learning. Thus, the increasingly widespread acceptance of this understanding of how learning actually occurs provides a strong evidentiary base for the dissolution – or at least blurring – of historical boundaries between sectors and providers, and lays the groundwork for a system of lifelong learning based on the triple pillars of 'learning to learn', the widespread availability of needed information and resources, and access to support and guidance.

New technologies and the digital revolution

The story of the spread of information and communication technologies (ICT), and their intrusion into many aspects of everyday life, is too well known to need repeating here. Even their incorporation into the world of teaching and learning has been exhaustively documented in a seemingly endless stream of books, articles, reports, conference papers, forums, blogs and other media.

Regrettably, however, a great deal of this literature in relation to technologically supported learning simply accepts uncritically existing assumptions about the nature of knowledge and of learning, and consequently reproduces conventional educational paradigms: 'e-mimicking' or reproducing in cyberspace established approaches to teaching and learning. This, however, represents an impoverished way of using such potentially powerful and emancipatory technologies, which have the capability to put learners and enquirers in touch not only with effectively limitless amounts of information and opinion, but also with experts and other learners throughout the world.

Viewed in this way, ICT is much more than simply a delivery mechanism for large volumes of predetermined information. It has the potential to help us to achieve the vision of lifelong learning; if not for all, then at least for an increasing proportion of the world's population, notably those who speak English, have access to reasonably high bandwidth and necessary technology, and have a degree of both technology literacy and information literacy.

But even in more conventional educational settings, such as education and training, ICT has the potential to blur and possibly even to obviate boundaries: between disciplines, between countries, between 'levels' of learning, between 'theory' and 'practice', even between teachers and learners. ICT, when wisely used, has the potential to support a lifelong learning agenda for learners of all ages, in all sorts of settings and contexts, with all sorts of learning goals and preferred modalities. For further information on this theme, see my recent report to the Australian government: *Linking Thinking: Self-Directed Learning in the Digital Age* (Candy 2004).

Lifelong learning networks: An idea whose time has passed?

It seems, then, that lifelong learning as a policy objective is enjoying something of a resurgence, and that it is supported by certain contextual changes that might enhance the likelihood if its succeeding. It is interesting to note, therefore, that in June 2004 the Learning and Skills Council (LSC) and the Higher Education Funding Council for England (HEFCE) jointly announced the creation of lifelong learning networks: regionally based consortia of higher and further education institutions that collaborate to:

- combine the strengths of a number of diverse institutions;
- provide support for learners on vocational pathways;
- bring greater clarity, coherence and certainty to progression opportunities;
- develop the curriculum as appropriate to facilitate progression;
- value vocational learning outcomes and provide opportunities for vocational learners to build on earlier learning; and
- *locate the progression strategy within a commitment to lifelong learning, ensuring that learners have access to a range of progression opportunities so that they can move between different kinds of vocational and academic programmes as their interests, needs and abilities develop.* (HEFCE 2004 (emphasis added))

This is, of course, a highly laudable initiative, which strives simultaneously to balance the needs of national coordination, of regional or local responsiveness, and of the learning trajectories of individual learners. It is however hardly unprecedented. Indeed it is remarkably reminiscent of the decision taken in November 2002 by the Strategic Learning and Research Advisory Group (StLaR) of the Departments of Health and for Education and Skills, to create regionally based 'health and education strategic partnerships' (HESPS) whose role, according to a joint communiqué issued by the Permanent Secretaries of both departments, would be:

to ensure effective joint working and strategic planning at the interface between health and social care, research and learning – mirroring the role of StLaR, but at a local level; they would be broadly based – reflecting all the relevant sectors, such as both Further and Higher Education; membership would be at a senior level – Chief Executives and other acknowledged local leaders; they would set their own local agenda, tackling issues relevant to all the partners; and they would strike a balance between tackling pressing problems and considering longer term strategic issues. (Department of Health 2004 (emphasis added))

Of course, HESPs are focused on the twin domains of health and education, whereas 'lifelong learning partnerships', which had been established a few years earlier, in 1999, had a much broader membership base:

Learning Partnerships are non-statutory, voluntary groupings of local learning providers (ranging from voluntary sector to Higher Education Institutes) and others such as local education authorities, Connexions/Careers Service, trade unions, employers and faith groups. They were established in order to provide a single strategic body in each area that would bring together all the existing local arrangements covering post-16 education and lifelong learning. *The intention to introduce local strategic partnerships to develop new approaches for the education and training of young people and adults was an aim of the incoming Labour government in 1997.* (Department for Education and Skills 2003 (emphasis added))

These two initiatives – HESPs and lifelong learning partnerships – in turn have more than a passing similarity to the Regional Development Agencies which were established in 1998 by the Department of Trade and Industry as non-departmental public bodies with a primary role as strategic drivers for regional economic development. Under the Regional Development Agencies Act 1998, each agency has five statutory purposes, which are:

- to further economic development and regeneration;
- to promote business efficiency, investment and competitiveness;
- to promote employment;
- to enhance development and application of skill relevant to employment; and
- to contribute to sustainable development.

Not unexpectedly, one of the principal levers available to RDAs to achieve these various aims was education and training, and as a result, they used the Skills Development Fund, for the purpose of:

- developing basic skills in the workplace;
- implementing key skills qualifications;
- developing IT in the workforce;
- using innovative approaches to methods of work-based learning;
- increasing the take-up and completion of Modern Apprenticeships;
- *raising participation in employment, lifelong learning and attainment among ethnic minority groups and disabled people* (Department of Trade and Industry 2001 (emphasis added))

It may thus be seen that these various government initiatives, all implemented since 1998, have very similar and in some cases identical objectives and memberships. But even this does not exhaust the range of regionally focused interventions with a concern for lifelong learning: there are also many local strategies as well that have a focus on promoting lifelong learning and collaboration between and among education and training providers. Many of these are covered by the Learning Cities Network (now subsumed under the Department for Education and Skills), and its pan-European counterpart, Towards a Learning Society, which:

> *encourages interactions between everyone with an interest in pursuing learning city development ambitions, instillers of lifelong learning as part of our society development, and promoters of collaboration between cities and their local initiatives in the areas of lifelong learning and learning society development.* The membership includes city managers, managers of learning institutions, lifelong learning facilitators, teachers, lecturers, other professionals who have the ambition to create an environment where learning takes place naturally and where human potential is nurtured. It is international in its scope and will lead to the practical exchange of ideas, experiences, good practice examples as well as the creative development of new collaborations, activities and initiatives. (Learning Cities Network 2001 (emphasis added))

My purpose in briefly recapitulating these various initiatives is to emphasise that lifelong learning networks have a number of precursors, both government-sponsored and community-based. While this should give comfort to those who believe that this approach is on the right track, the fact that there are so many parallel schemes should sound a note of caution about yet another initiative which is to be superimposed on a policy environment already replete with many similar ideas and programmes.

Where does all this leave us?

Clearly, the concept of some kind of regional or local partnership between further and higher education institutions to promote and advance lifelong learning is an inherently desirable idea, as demonstrated – if by nothing else – by the number of recent attempts to achieve this. But the very fact that so few of these initiatives seem to have led to dramatically enhanced learning opportunities should act as a caution against unbridled optimism and as a stimulus towards lateral thinking about what might have been missing from previous attempts.

It is the basic premise of this paper that there are now circumstances in place that could perhaps facilitate the long-sought realisation of lifelong learning opportunities, and which might mitigate the factors that have prevented this in the past. However, for lifelong learning networks to be demonstrably more effective than other similar ideas, it is vital for advocates to:

1. Take account of the aims (and imposts) of extant lifelong learning programmes

In practice, it is likely to be the same organisations – and indeed even the same people within those organisations – who are involved in implementing the lifelong learning networks as have been primarily implicated in other parallel attempts to create lifelong learning in particular regions. Rather than reinventing the wheel, or adding a further burden onto those who are already heavily loaded, therefore, it would probably be wise to ascertain what lifelong learning partnerships, agreements, networks and projects already exist in any given locale, and to build on them, rather than create something *ab initio*.

Linked to this is the often ignored piece of advice that, since lifelong learning projects are for the benefit of learners, the learners themselves should be involved from the outset in designing approaches that are ostensibly for their benefit. Successful interventions are usually based on partnerships with their beneficiaries, rather than well-meaning but often paternalistic impositions on them.

2. Support learning rather than teaching

Despite an ostensible commitment to lifelong *learning*, many interventions – even well-intentioned ones – are actually concerned with teaching instead. Their principal objective is to increase participation and enrolment in formal courses. While they seem to exhibit an enlightened attitude towards facilitating transfer between institutions, and even between sectors, they tacitly reinforce existing institutional paradigms. If the lifelong learning networks are to be truly effective, they need to begin by taking the perspective of the learner, or the would-be learner, and concentrating on providing the kind of information, advice, guidance and support such a person might want.

Such help should, in the first instance, probably be made available in non-institutional settings such as workplaces, libraries and community centres. It should include the creation and development of learning support groups, and should be organised according to the needs and interests of learners rather than the administrative convenience or conventional disciplinary structures of formal education; it might be useful to think in terms of an analogy – a 'travel agency for the mind' in a high street location, similar to the highly successful Learning Shop in Norwich.

Finally, such approaches should provide an opportunity for those returning to formal study after a break to obtain credit for relevant life experience. Accordingly, it would be desirable to assist such people to create learning portfolios with a view to gaining accreditation of prior learning (APL) – both credentialled and uncredentialled.

3. Take account of the impacts of technology on available information and learning contexts

Conventional wisdom holds that we are only at the very early stages of incorporating technology seamlessly into our lives, although clearly this varies markedly according to age, gender, socio-economic status, geographic location, prior educational attainment and so on. One needs only to observe the prevalence of mobile phone use in public places and the number of (predominantly) young people who seem perfectly at home with technologies (ATMs, video recorders, Palm Pilots, digital cameras, etc.) to realise that there is a generational shift occurring in technology use.

Moreover, technology can be used a lot more creatively to support learners than is currently the case. Innovators such as Ultralab at Anglia Polytechnic University are leading the way, for instance through their 'NotSchool' Project, in engaging alienated, marginalised and disenfranchised young people in learning. Commercial enterprises such as Amazon.com are creating both online communities and more engaged users through the clever use of 'push technology'. Lobby groups, community forums and interest groups are using technology in ingenious and creative ways to develop genuinely engaging online communities where people are free to exchange information and opinions.

The convergence of more ubiquitous, user friendly and robust technology with a genuine determination to empower people as learners could well herald a whole new era in terms of lifelong learning, which could at last become, as envisaged by Faure and his colleagues thirty years ago, 'the master concept for educational policies in the years to come for both developed and developing countries' (Faure 1972, p. 182).

References

Candy, Philip C. (2004) *Linking Thinking: Self-Directed Learning in the Digital Age*, DEST Research Fellowship Scheme Report. Canberra: Department of Education, Science and Training. Available online at http://www.dest.gov.au/research/publications/linking_thinking/report.pdf (accessed 12 January 2005).

Department for Education and Skills (DfES) (2003) *Education Departments: Learning Partnerships*. Available online at http://ndad.ulcc.ac.uk/CRDA/53/detail.html (accessed 12 January 2005).

Department of Health (DoH) (2004) *Joint Letter from Department of Health and Department for Education and Skills: Health and Education Strategic Partnerships*. Available online at http://www.dh.gov.uk/assetRoot/04/01/38/67/04013867.pdf (accessed 12 January 2005).

Department of Trade and Industry (DTI) (2001) *England's Regional Development Agencies: Transforming England's Regions through Sustainable Economic Development*. Available online at http://www.consumer.gov.uk/rda/info/ (accessed 12 January 2005).

Faure, Edgar (Chairman) (1972) *Learning To Be: The World of Education Today and Tomorrow*, Report of the International Commission on the Future of Education. Paris: Unesco.

Higher Education Funding Council for England (HEFCE) (2004) *Joint Letter from HEFCE and the Learning and Skills Council: HEFCE Circular Letter number 12/2004*. Available online at http://www.hefce.ac.uk/pubs/ circlets/2004/cl12_04/ (accessed 12 January 2005).

Learning Cities Network (2001). *Towards a Learning Society*. Available online at http://newtels.euproject.org/go.cfm?PageId=777 (accessed 12 January 2005).

CHAPTER THREE

Prospects for adult learning in higher education

Richard Taylor

Introduction

There are currently several fundamental policy issues in British higher education, and the short to medium future remains as volatile as ever. This chapter, appropriately, perhaps, prepared for a NIACE seminar, concentrates on one of them: what are the prospects for adult learning and adult learners in higher education?[1]

The chapter takes the following form:

(i)   the context for analysing this question, focusing, first, on the negative aspects at both macro and micro levels and, second, on the positives;
(ii) a brief discussion (or rather series of assertions) about the broad values, and thus objectives, which should characterise the advocacy of adult learners' interests in the higher education policy arena;
(iii) the politics of the current policy debate in relation to adult learning/ learners and the 'pressure points' upon which to concentrate.

Context

Negative factors
At the societal level, the growth of an individualistic culture, with the corollary of the virtual collapse of collectivist (although arguably not of community) perspectives, has many negative consequences; the most relevant, in the context of this paper, are that it has undermined the networking structure and the general appeal of adult education. There has been a rapid de-industrialisation of the British economy, as a result both of the irrationalities of global capitalism and of the particular neo-liberal politics promulgated with zeal by Margaret Thatcher and her successors, including, of course, Tony Blair. This has been in part cause and in part effect of the culture of individualism; and it is also connected with the decline of working-class communities (cf. Hoggart 1957; Williams 1961, 1979) and the corresponding trivialisation of the media and popular culture (Anderson 2004).

Politically, the systematic erosion of Labour's modest social democratic reformism by New Labour has had a number of negative effects in the field in question, as in virtually all other areas of policy and ideology. As I have argued at length elsewhere, New Labour's approach to lifelong learning can be characterised as 'marketised welfarism'. It is thus not merely Thatcherism in new clothes, but an uneasy amalgam of a number of ideological strands, including commitments to concepts of equality of opportunity, meritocracy and individualism (Taylor forthcoming 2005). The relevant negativities of New Labour in the context of the prospects for adult learners and learning may be summarised as follows.

First, an almost exclusive concentration upon 'human capital' arguments for the expansion of education, especially higher education: the fallacies inherent in this perspective, at least when pursued to the exclusion of all else, have been demonstrated repeatedly by critics, notably Frank Coffield (Coffield 1999).

Second, despite all the evidence of increasing diversities within the higher education system – of age, of mode, of awards, and so on – government has focused upon young (18–21) people undertaking full-time, three-year honours degree programmes, who are resident at a university distant from their home.[2]

Third, and perhaps most serious of all, government has combined an emphasis upon an instrumental vocationalism with a de facto commitment to a 'sheep and goats' system: that is, the vocational emphasis is concentrated at sub-degree level (foundation degrees *et al.*) at the post-1992 universities and delivered in partnership with further education, while the 'elite' universities are encouraged to pursue their research and 18–21 full-time agenda. Guess where adult learners fit in? Nothing has been done – rather the reverse – to dismantle the hierarchy of higher education institutions or to begin to introduce funding and other structures which address 'fitness for purpose' criteria.

There are, finally, on the negatives list, several particular aspects of current policy which are detrimental to the interests of adult learners and adult learning.

First, of course, there is the 'top-up fees' system: enough has been said on this but, clearly, this will deter both adult learners (especially the over-55s) who most often wish to study part-time and, more generally, it will deter working-class students as a whole.

Second, government has done nothing, beyond rhetorical exhortation, to ensure that employers contribute to the costs of their employees' education and training (Tuckett 2000; Taylor forthcoming 2005).

Third, for a variety of reasons, both the outreach, community education provision of institutions and, in the pre-1992 part of the sector, most of the dedicated departments/schools/centres for adult and continuing education, have been abolished, or severely reduced in size and function.

Fourth, there has been an increasing tendency, which was evident before the advent of the Labour government in 1997, to equate worthwhile learning with modules and programmes which carry appropriate certification. Many adult learners do not want or need certification; moreover, because only this provision attracts public funding, innovative and flexible programming, including outreach work, becomes all but impossible.

Finally, less tangibly, the research agenda in the field of adult learning and lifelong learning has tended to concentrate upon the quantitative study of process and structures as opposed, for example, to analyses of the trans-formative potential of lifelong learning, and the connections between adult education and social purpose.

Positive factors

This is a pretty bleak picture. What is there on the sunny side? Some of the positive points are obvious. The overall expansion of the higher education system, and the drive towards widening participation, have both benefited adult learners, albeit more often by default than intent. There are clearly many more adult learners in higher education than ever before. The blurring of sectoral boundaries and the development of much wider and more flexible structures of provision and awards are also of obvious benefit to adult learners.

Perhaps justifying rather more discussion are several other factors:

- the implications of regional structures and agendas;
- trans-European opportunities in the enlarged European community;
- demographic trends.

In terms, first, of the regional agenda, however stuttering and confused its purpose, this seems certain to develop, and equally certain to have an emphasis upon education and training with a lifelong learning orientation. This will be – is – again focused on skills development and related opportun-ities deriving from the human capital agenda; but there is a real opportunity here for developing a reoriented social purpose and community education provision by working with the citizenship programme. This may be a means of revivifying the sadly dormant tradition of (radical) social and political education, although there is much work to be done in terms of LSC culture, let alone that of the regional development authorities (RDAs).

Trans-European credit transfer systems are in their infancy in terms of *practice* but the likely growth of labour and cultural migration, and general short- to medium-term labour mobility across the new Europe, plus the complementary growth of distance learning via the internet, are likely to result in increased opportunities for adult learners, especially in the post-experience, continuing professional development (CPD) area. Again, there are possibili-ties here for building on social and political European agendas for education, and in a rather different context, anti-racist, environmental and other progressive pan-European social movements.

Finally, policy-makers have eventually recognised the gravity of demo-graphic projections in Britain and most, though not all, European countries, and the implications these have for lifelong learning, extended often part-time working lives, and the largely untapped resource of ever growing numbers of retired people with both specific and generic skills. There is a huge agenda here for lifelong learning in all sectors; adult educators have a virtually blank sheet, though not as yet a blank cheque, to work upon.

All this adds up to a potentially positive agenda. Whether or not it can be realised depends, as ever, very largely on ideological and political questions, rather than economic or educational ones. What are the values and the political agendas that, as educators, we should be advocating?

Values and political agendas for adult learning in higher education

There is a substantial literature devoted to such questions. As noted at the outset, the intention here is to sketch a series of assertions that seem to me relevant to the present context.

The starting-points for those advocating adult learning, especially in higher education, are twofold: first, a recognition that, for wider structural reasons, there are very large numbers of adults who have not had the opportunity to benefit from any relevant and accessible education and training since the end of their compulsory schooling. A high priority has to be to engage as many as possible of such potential learners. Second, as far as higher education is concerned, adult learning is centred on developing an open-ended, rigorous, critical and sceptical approach to academic study. Complementing these two core beliefs are two others: that pedagogy, curriculum and mode should be developed in partnership with individual learners and with the communities of interest from which they come, rather than being determined by often conservative and inward-looking institutions and their academic staff; secondly, that this critical, liberal and responsive approach should be sector-wide – that is, not restricted, as is largely the case at present, to the 'elite' institutions and their predominantly young middle-class students.

Just to outline such a value framework illustrates how distant are the present politics of higher education. Ideologically, the contemporary context is characterised by the post-Thatcherite, but distinctively different, perspective of New Labour. The climate is highly volatile, however, and – ever the optimist – my view is that assuming Labour wins the 2005 election the ideological tenor of the New Labour government will signal at least a partial retreat from the zealous modernising of the present Prime Minister. The reasons for this volatility and likely change in orientation of course have nothing to do with lifelong learning or higher education per se, but are part of the much wider canvas of New Labour's political crisis – Iraq *et al.* Be that as it may, this political weakness and the forthcoming General Election campaign perhaps offer more chance of achieving policy shifts in the interests of adult learning than has been the case for the last seven years of the New Labour government.

Policy pressure points for advocates of lifelong learning

Assuming that the value position described above is one which others in the adult learning community are happy to sign up to, where are the short-term policy pressure points to be found?

The new higher education lifelong learning networks (LLNs), initiated by the Higher Education Funding Council for England (HEFCE), are clearly a potentially important policy structure here. We should engage with them as fully as possible and make every effort to develop them, in as much as they are beneficial for adult learners. I have two concerns, however. The more minor one is the danger that they will be – or will be perceived to be – yet another otiose bureaucratic networking structure. There is, after all, a plethora of such bodies already, mostly spanning the whole post-compulsory sector, in which higher education is only one player. Moreover, higher education institutions, and individual academic staff, have many other pressing concerns. LLNs will have to be 'sold' effectively if they are to be taken seriously by the field. What specific and useful purpose do they have? And, inevitably, are there significant resources attached potentially to development work undertaken?

The more important issue is the proposed remit of the LLNs. Recent papers, including one discussed in September 2004 at HEFCE's Strategic Advisory Committee for Widening Participation, made it clear that the intention is that the networks should concentrate only upon vocational provision for young learners. Clearly, this is an important area; equally clearly, the networks must have focus if they are to succeed. Nevertheless, such an orientation is a travesty of a real commitment to lifelong learning: we should do everything we can, not to oppose the new networks and their functions, but to develop rapidly the more transformative adult learning perspective outlined here. How susceptible HEFCE will be to such a perspective is debatable, but the first step must be to lobby through the field and its organisations, not least NIACE. In this context, too, we can draw on NIACE's detailed surveys of adult learners' participation, which show worrying trends developing.

Two other high-profile innovations that adult learning advocates should work on are the inequitable treatment of adult learning and part-time higher education under the terms of the new Higher Education Act, and the way in which the remit of the new Office for Fair Access (OFFA) Access Regulator will be articulated. These are both susceptible to further pressure.[3] The problems in this case seem to stem more from cock-up than conspiracy. There has been a cultural blind-spot about all learners in higher education except standard 18–21-year-olds, and, falling a long way behind, an acknowledgement that vocational provision through foundation degrees and the like are important as ancillary provision for dealing with the intermediate skills gap. There are, then, real prospects of achieving modest advance over the term of the next government on adult learning issues such as the age cap at 55. Similarly, OFFA's remit has now been broadened to include consideration of access for part-time learners; more might be achieved by working closely with the Access Regulator and the associated officers.

As sectoral boundaries become more blurred, we can develop more partnerships for adult learning with further education, and with the LSC more generally. Aimhigher already has a structure and a good record in this area. Perhaps we can extend this model and look towards a flexible partnership with the voluntary sector – for example, over the demographic issues noted earlier.

Linked to this latter area, among others, is the opportunity for more targeted research, much of it commissioned by public bodies. Not only should individual academics and research groups in universities look to tender for such work, bodies such as UACE and NIACE can extend the job they already do to coordinate research activity across a range of institutions.

Finally, one damaging and widespread phenomenon in recent years in the pre-1992 university sector has been the closure or drastic diminution in size and function of dedicated departments of adult and continuing education. In some cases, such departments had failed to adjust to radically changed circumstances; and similarly, in some cases, there were real concerns about standards, appropriateness of provision and research capacity. Nevertheless, such widespread destruction of those best equipped and most committed to adult learning is a significant setback both to the government's lifelong learning agenda and to the emphasis upon regionalism and cross-sector working. It is salutary and in some ways encouraging to hear the frequently expressed concern and surprise of ministers and other senior policy-makers when informed of such negative developments. While this is partly a matter of intra-institutional politics, it also reflects the ways in which national funding formulae and bureaucratic structures discriminate against adult learning provision. Through our national organisations we should lobby for appropriate changes.

Very few people are likely to be excited or energised by the return of a third Labour government. We might hope for a diminution in the influence of New Labour ideology and a return to the modestly redistributive domestic policies that previously characterised Labourism. If this is to be the tenor of the third term, there are prospects for modest advance for adult learners' interests: hardly a rallying cry to set the blood coursing, but still worth pursuing, not least because it may offer space to develop the longer-term 'social purpose' agendas.

Notes

1   By adult learners, I mean those over the age of 21 who have had a significant break between completing full-time education and their entry into higher education.

2   The reasons for this, I would hazard, are in part to do with human capital assumptions and, in part, cultural, in that their own higher education – three years' full-time study away from home at a young age in an 'elite' institution – is the common experience of both leading politicians and senior civil servants.

3   NIACE has shown already how much can be achieved for adult learners
    through effective briefings and lobbying.

References

Anderson, Perry (2004) *London Review of Books*.
Coffield, Frank (1999) *Breaching the Consensus: Lifelong Learning as Social Control*,
    Inaugural Lecture, February. Newcastle: University of Newcastle.
Coffield, Frank (1999) *Why is the Beer always Stronger up North? Studies of Lifelong
    Learning in Europe*. London: Policy Press.
Hoggart, Richard (1957) *The Uses of Literacy*. London: Pelican.
Taylor, Richard (forthcoming, spring 2005) *Lifelong Learning and the Labour
    Governments 1997–2004*, Special Edition, *Oxford Review of Education*.
Tuckett, Alan (2000) 'Why don't employers pay their way?', *Guardian*, 10 May
    2000.
Williams, Raymond (1961) *The Long Revolution*. London: Pelican.
Williams, Raymond (1979) *Politics and Letters*. London: Verso.

CHAPTER FOUR

Further and higher education: A cautionary note

Adrian Perry

Every American college president, it appears, is duty bound to write and utter at least one book upon the nature and usufructs of higher education. . . . As a rule he puts it off till his autumn days, when the hemlock of senility has begun to dull the edge of his troubles, but he seldom dodges it altogether. I have on my shelves a long row of such books, and I have read them all with a respectful and hopeful spirit, for I think I may call myself, without vanity, a fan of learned men. But I must add, in all honesty, that I have yet to find in any such tome anything properly describable as wisdom. (H. L. Mencken, 'The boon of culture', American Mercury, September 1931)

Any discussion about the future and purposes of further education colleges should start by pointing out the differences between the members of the collective we lump together as further education (FE). Let's leave sixth form colleges aside for the purposes of this discussion: they are what David Melville once described as 'one of the great success stories of British education', and plainly have a strong interest in preparation for higher education. Specialist colleges – land-based, art – also enjoy clear articulation. The adult colleges are successful in blending non-vocational adult education with university access. But even beyond these categories, there are marked differences between FE colleges. Some cater predominantly for 16–19-year-olds, others for adults.[1] Some are sharply focused on the labour market: the Centres of Vocational Excellence articulate clearly with employer needs. Others who stress a community mission, with an emphasis towards basic skills, work with students with learning disabilities and difficulties (LDD) and the teaching of English as a second or other language (ESOL). That is why any general thesis on 'What is the role of FE in HE expansion?' is never an easy question to answer. Having said that, there are plenty of good reasons why a study of wider participation in higher education might include a chapter on the FE system.

First, the colleges have great potential as the source of new entrants into universities. It is generally agreed that the expansion of higher education cannot come from recruiting more successful sixth form students: almost all 18-year-olds achieving good level-3 qualifications already enter higher education. The role of FE is particularly important if HE expansion is to come from higher vocational qualifications. Foundation degrees may have made a halting start, but the creation of a respected basic HE qualification, with a vocational flavour, is an important task. After all, most of the workforce of 2020 is made up of adults who are at work now.

In some areas, a link with higher education is essential. Take, for example, the health and social care sector, where colleges have a large and growing commitment to training. Though the bulk of the provision is at lower levels, it is important to articulate with the degree-level qualifications that are needed for professional-level jobs. This is not just for progression opportunities. Training will be better for including the full range of workers in an industry, to share a common understanding of new developments, and ensure that skills and systems used at various levels overlap and connect. The media world, too, demands graduate and higher technician skills.

Second, the colleges can provide higher education opportunities themselves. The Scots have a higher participation in higher education, already nearing the 50 per cent target that some English commentators regard as utopian. But they achieve that by providing much of the higher technician work in their further education colleges. Further education can present a strong case for a growing role in HE expansion south of the border. The new entrants will often be part-time students, wanting to study part-time and close to home; they may regard the 'experience of higher education' as an extension of their vocational studies at the local college. This is particularly true in subject areas – like dental technology, construction or catering – where an FE institution shows strong expertise. In rural areas, higher education may only be accessible for those with work or family commitments in the local college. And, to speak realistically, the rising costs of higher education might begin to favour a local, low-cost producer.

Third, the college system has the skills and experience to reach the new learner. Placed in their communities, it attracts many more students than the university sector does – often from working-class and ethnic minority communities who have not benefited from the traditional school and university offer. Recent HEFCE research shows just how much help the university sector needs before it can consider itself at all inclusive. But it is not just a matter of class or ethnicity. FE has rich experience of meeting the needs of students who are mixing study with the demands of home and work. There is a tradition of progression – people joining for a low-level course with no ambition of higher-level study, but moving to higher-level work as their confidence and interest grows.

Game, set and match, then. FE needs to be energised to help with the HE targets – end of story. Or is it? There are, in my view, reasons to be cautious before rushing to that conclusion.

The main worry is mission drift – that an emphasis on HE links will pull FE colleges away from the important work for the bulk of their clients – which is technician studies, basic education and ESOL, and employer-related skills. It is, after all, in the area of technician skills that the UK falls furthest from international standards: this is shown in Figure 4.1. It is a strange irony that the UK discourse about the challenge of globalisation and skills turns easily into worries about school standards and the production of graduates. In fact, our production of graduates (as opposed to participation in HE – not the same thing at all) is not shamefully short of international norms. And OECD surveys indicate that the problem with UK school standards is not the absolute level – there have been a number of years where our youngsters have merited comparison with the best – but one of equity. Where we do have a problem is in the long tail of very poorly performing young people.

These are precisely the people that FE is increasingly working with: they are the group which poses the greatest challenges. It was striking how the Ofsted publication *Why Colleges Succeed* showed a range of colleges working overwhelmingly at level 3, whereas the companion document *Why Colleges Fail* featured many institutions working with level 1 and 2 young people. Getting it right for this lost generation – the very school products whose grasp of basic skills makes employers despair – is noble and desperately important work. It is an effort where university linkages are the least relevant. Indeed, they could be counter-productive. I have worked in institutions where the prestige and attractiveness of higher-level work has dragged resource and attention away from key groups: at one extreme, a college in a tough inner-city borough where the engineering department ran a range of HNC evening classes but no full-time provision below level 3. As a result, they had nothing to offer two-thirds of local school-leavers.

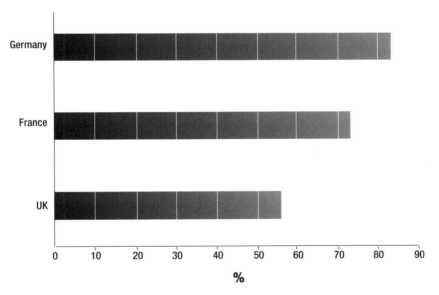

Figure 4.1 Qualifications at level 2+ in France, Germany and the UK, 1998.
Source: Skills Task Force (2000).

The poor prospects for this group may be linked to our lack of a strong and respected system of vocational preparation. This is the Government's view, and lies behind the 14–16 flexibility projects and the renewed emphasis on apprenticeship. We certainly need to do something. I noted above that it is actually in technician qualifications that we fall furthest behind our global competitors. This is where the effort needs to be put, with colleges and work-based providers getting closer to employers both in vocational work for 16–19-year-olds, and in upskilling adults in the labour force. This work fits the FE ethic well, for it combines the sector's two dominant values: increasing skills for the labour market, and a commitment to greater equity.

	UK	Germany
Top 40 per cent	12.35	12.86
Next 20 per cent	6.00	8.25
Bottom 40 per cent	3.68	5.64

Table 4.1 Wage rates in Germany and the UK (£ per hr)
Source: Layard, Macintosh and Vignoles 2002.

Table 4.1 shows that those at the upper end of the labour market are paid as well as those in a similar position in Germany. However, the gap stretches out at the bottom end of the labour market. So increasing the spread of skills to international levels holds the promise of not merely reducing skills shortages, but also increasing equality for the low paid. This isn't necessarily about long courses that lead to qualifications. Short, punchy work with employer-led groups will form an increasingly important part of a campaign to raise skills and productivity. As with under-qualified 16-year-olds, however, there is a major challenge in meeting the needs of adults with poor qualifications, shown in Figure 4.2.

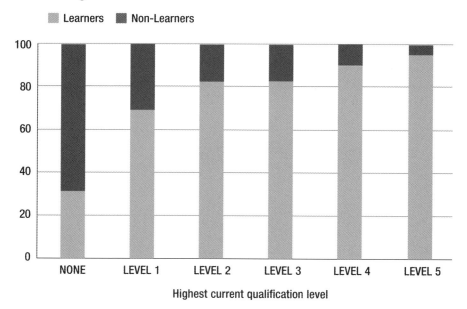

Figure 4.2 Percentage of learners and non-learners by highest current qualification.
Source: DFES, *National Adult Learning Survey* 2001.

This shows that access to education and training is a bigger problem for those with no, or few, qualifications. It is worth remembering that this means 35 per cent or more of the workforce. As with young people, it is this group to whom university linkages and the prospect of higher education offer least. This does not mean FE colleges should steer clear of participation in HE expansion. They are used to balancing the needs of a broad cohort of learners – low level and high, vocational and academic, young and adult. But resources and management attention are finite: prioritisation means choosing what not to do as well as what to do. Figure 4.2 makes it hard to argue that the overwhelming consideration should be providing more opportunities for those at level 3.

The fact is that most people entering FE do not wish to go to university. Many, perhaps most, are indeed planning to gain a qualification for career advancement. But this may not call for connections to HE: in areas like construction, for example, the level-4 provision is in advanced craft and site management. And elsewhere motivation is in fact more complex than is sometimes thought. Vocational ambitions are not always about applying for the next level up in a given job: people want to open up access to new areas of work. Just look at the explosion of counselling courses as an example. Career exploration is widespread: a survey for the Central London Learning and Skills Council found that more than half the FE students who had been taking a course the previous year had changed their programme area. Others study for interest, wanting to master digital imaging or Spanish or economics or first aid or a hundred other subjects and skills. Social motivations are important too, and go way beyond the women's magazine advice to join an evening class to avoid loneliness: for many people, a college course is an early marker in a rebuilt life.

The idea that a college course is the start of getting a grip on one's life is nowhere more important than in the case of students improving their basic skills. Literacy, numeracy and English as a second or other language form a substantial part of modern college provision. There are some inner-city colleges where it actually forms the bulk of the work. The Moser Report indicated that 7 million Britons lacked the literacy or numeracy skills to operate effectively in a modern economy and in their personal life. The way forward here is surely to link our 'social rescue' programmes – not just Skills for Life, but also unemployment retraining – with agencies like the housing associations, Job Centre Plus and the welfare system, and ideally with progressive employers. This aligns college work with government ambitions to get people off welfare and into work. Links with higher education might be appropriate for some of our first-level learners – particularly ESOL students for whom English language skills present the last major barrier to a university place or professional job. But for most of them, this isn't the case, and it would be sad to regard this important national work as a subordinate activity in the great drive to expand HE.

To summarise where we have got to, then. Arguments have been deployed that ask FE to take a large role in expanding higher education. It plainly has a contribution to make – in accessing and preparing non-traditional learners, and in progression within the lower vocational curriculum. But I have argued that the major tasks that FE faces are not in HE expansion. They involve upskilling those in work and meeting the needs of adults and young people who have got little from the emphasis on schools standards. Some of these client groups will look to higher education. Others, perhaps the majority, will not. The awkward question is surely – when 50 per cent have higher education experience, what happens to the other half? Talk of a 'lifelong, inclusive system of tertiary education' may leave them cold.

Which is where a final (and to managers and governors perhaps most seductive) reason for the involvement of the further education colleges in HE expansion comes in. It is that engagement with universities and the prestige of the higher education world might strengthen and energise a sector which has traditionally been at the back of the educational queue.[2] The usual reasons for the feeling that FE is the poor relation – tighter budgets than schools and universities, inability to own the qualification base, government preference for school sixth forms and private sector providers, a general invisibility in educational discourse – have recently been supplemented by demands for choice and contestability.[3] The Skills Strategy showed its newly discovered enthusiasm for vocational skills by picking at the shortcomings of those who have long been engaged in this work. The development of a distinctive 14–19 curriculum, the freedom of schools to open new sixth form provision, and the desire for expanded numbers in HE could leave FE colleges as marginal providers, engaged in client groups and educational provision with which other, more favoured, institutions choose not to work. Two recent White Papers have required FE colleges to reconsider their mission. So has the LSC's *Agenda for Change*, which curiously asks FE to 'look at distinctive contribution/ realign their own institutions in the context *against* which colleges operate' (my emphasis). In the current context, it could plausibly be argued that colleges aren't able to decide their mission: it is simply a residual. It may be good PR to describe the sector as 'education's adaptive layer' but this does not conceal a worry that the sector will increasingly exist in the crannies of the educational landscape. Tony Henry, one of the sector's more thoughtful as well as amusing Principals, recently gave a speech on 'The Death of FE': he was only half-joking.

In this context, some friends of FE argue that a strong link with universities will provide a better public image, more progression for students and greater control over the curriculum. The sheen of university-level work might burnish the college even where the actual proportion of provision involving HE links is small: American community colleges are regarded as part of the higher education system even though in places like New York very few of their students are engaged on undergraduate work.

This argument is pretty novel. It starts from a view that FE is worth having, and the HE system needs to be shaped to help it achieve its purposes and targets rather than vice versa. What is needed if this approach is to succeed?

The first aspect must involve the FE sector having much more control of the design and accreditation of qualifications than is the case at the moment. This should start with foundation degrees,[4] but need not stop there. Universities have credibility in qualifications: they could help FE construct an escape route from the expensive mess that is the UK vocational awards system. This implies a role beyond what is conventionally described as higher education. For example, they might well be able to accredit the customised provision that FE will increasingly wish to deliver to small and medium-sized enterprises. And wouldn't it be great if students with learning difficulties were able to attain a university certificate? The key question will be whether the universities could actually deliver the responsiveness needed at an acceptable cost.

The second element is partnership based on equality and respect. Some excellent examples – Staffordshire, Kent – already exist. There are some signals that would show this in practice – such as joint management of shared facilities, and franchise arrangements whose financial provisions directed resources to the poorer partner. Universities need to be sensitive to the power of predation, recognising that it is in their own interest not to strip local FE colleges of their best work. My own feeling is that these sorts of relationships are probably best built one-on-one: wider partnership can have benefits in establishing shared guidance and admissions paths, but can become cumbersome and inflexible.

HE support will not be enough. FE needs to gain the confidence to shape its own agenda, with a more forceful marketing presence, greater flexibility, close engagement with the labour market and a determination to raise more of its own resources from its clients. If it succeeds, the benefits will be considerable. It is a sector that has been making a distinguished contribution to our educational progress in the past hundred years or more. Currently, it is the country's largest post-16 provider, with more learners than all the universities and sixth forms added together, and the major share of the £8 billion learning and skills budget. Well-led and well-supported, it could have a great role in the future. The important tasks are:

- providing job-ready entrants for the labour market;
- making a name for its ability to help employers improve the skills and attitudes of their workforce – especially at levels 2 and 3;
- cutting into the areas of skill gaps and shortages – such as management and supervisory skills, and increasingly higher-level IT – and into occupations poorly served by the training infrastructure, like logistics and retailing;

- continuing to deliver Skills For Life, and finding effective ways to reach the increasingly hard-to-reach groups needing to develop them;
- raising the attainment of the UK population by helping many more to enter universities, as well as shaping and delivering high-level technical training themselves.

If we can make sure that the sector's relationship with HE strengthens and supports these objectives, rather than diverts attention away from them, then we will have achieved a great deal.

Notes

1 In Central London, for example, the proportion of work made up by 16–19-year-old full-timers varies between 22 per cent in one college and virtually nil in another.
2 An interesting example of the relative power positions is to be found in the current Foster Review of FE. When Dearing was announced, higher education mobilised to consider the terms of reference, to vet and lobby the committee members, and generally played a major role in setting the agenda. FE has had (as far as I know) no input into the terms of reference – and there are no members to lobby.
3 The definition of contestability is revealing: the proposal is that new, and presumably private, providers be invited to tender for FE work, and that schools wanting to develop sixth forms should be allowed to. There is no suggestion that FE colleges might take over the work of local sixth forms, or capture LSC-funded work delivered by a nearby university.
4 If universities will not play, there is a case for an FE CNAA.

References

DfES (Department for Education and Skills) (annual) *National Adult Learning Survey*.

DfES (Department for Education and Skills) (2004) *Skills Strategy: Technical Evidence on Underlying Data and Evidence*.

Layard, Richard, S. McIntosh and A. Vignoles (2002) *Britain's Record on Skills*, Discussion Paper 23. London: Centre for the Economics of Education, LSE.

Learning and Skills Development Agency (LSDA) (2004) *21st Century Skills: Realising Our Potential* ('The Skills Strategy'), Cm. 5810. London: The Stationery Office.

McGaw, Barry (2003) *An International View of Policy Options and Trends*, address to LSDA Annual Conference. Paris: OECD.

National Skills Task Force (2000) *Skills for All: Proposals for a National Skills Agenda*, Final Report. London: The Stationery Office.
Ofsted (2004) *Why Colleges Succeed* and *Why Colleges Fail*.

CHAPTER FIVE

More of the same or radical change?

Geoff Layer

The debate about shifting to a concept of tertiary education is challenging at best, but within today's educational setting we need to be sure about what we are campaigning for and why. We have to be clear what we mean by tertiary, what it will deliver, and what difference it will make. The OECD seeks to analyse and interpret data on a comparative basis and therefore refers to tertiary as if it was an agreed and understood model. I am more concerned with understanding tertiary as a system and the benefits it could bring. Without the latter there is no point in taking it forward.

In 1984 I was a new resident in the city of Sheffield, a new lecturer at Sheffield City Polytechnic, a trade union activist and a member of the Labour Party. In the latter two roles I was thrown into the new debate across the city except we called it 'Post Primary Reorganisation' or by its shorter title – *tertiary*. This was an attempt to bring together the secondary schools, the five further education colleges and the ten separate adult education divisions into a coherent and planned structure for post-16 delivery across what turned out later to be six tertiary colleges. At the time the polytechnic was part of the local education authority and I used to go along to meetings and ask whether the 'Poly' was included in this model of post-primary or post-16 reorganisation. The answer from the pained officials was always that it was not meant to be included as the reorganisation didn't involve higher education. I tell this story simply to rehearse the argument that we need to be clear about what we mean by terminology as the 'Poly' was obviously post-primary and post-16, it just wasn't part of this landscape.

Having also spent two years engaged in negotiations with what turned out to be an unsuccessful merger proposal between a large college of further education and a university I am cautious over steps towards integration, especially if they are provider-led and provider-determined. The more radical and usually missing agenda is to approach the issue from a learner-driven perspective. While *tertiary* is an ideal I will gladly sign up to there is little evidence of either institutions or government seriously pursuing such a learner-driven agenda. The Further Education Funding Council may have argued that its demand-led entitlement was learner-driven before it was abolished due to its success and drain on resource. The truth of what really happened with this demand-led entitlement was that two existing providers of learning or training entered into arrangements to count some existing activity against the public purse. It was Tesco the employer that wanted its checkout assistants trained, not the individual learner clamouring to be empowered by the till.

If we assume for this seminar that the notion of tertiary is working across the further/higher education divide then we need to be equally sure that we understand those sectors and that there is sufficient common ground. It is important that the higher education (HE) agenda does not dominate the Lifelong Learning campaign merely because the Professors of Lifelong Learning are in the universities.

The progress and the uniqueness of further education is equally important. Most of what I will say is rooted in an experience of higher education, twenty years of being involved in the Open College movement, establishing Associate College Networks, four years in further education (FE) when it was very different from today, and a commitment to successfully widening participation in HE.

I have to start from a political and personal perspective, based on that experience:

- I do not believe NIACE should be campaigning for part-time *adult learners per se*. Students in HE are all over 18 and they all have jobs and study. This is a different form of pressure outside of study to part-time learners but we should not polarise the position of adult learners and assume they are a homogenous group. Times have changed and HE campuses look very different from the golden age of the buoyant extra-mural departments. NIACE should focus any campaign on adults being able to easily engage in learning, and providers being appropriately funded.
- We need to distinguish between returning to initial learning and continuing professional development in our arguments, as they need different campaigns.
- Current government policy is driven by economic need to such an extent that the 'social capitalists' are having to hang on in there.
- There is still a particular view of universities in Labour Party policy, which inhibits being radical through assuming hierarchies and elites.

The changing nature of the HE sector

There have been a number of significant changes within higher education in the UK over the last 20 years. In order to fully understand the argument put forward there is a need to look at a number of key issues in the development of higher education.

As Figure 5.1 demonstrates there has been steady growth in the sector since 1997, rising from under 500,000 first-year undergraduate students to nearly 700,000 in 2002/03.

There has also been a shift in the make-up of the student population. What used to be a male-dominated preserve has now shifted to the majority being

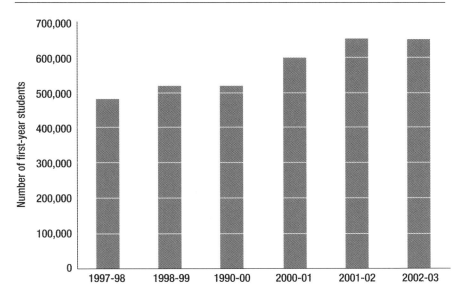

Figure 5.1 Number of first-year students. Source: HESA 1997-2003.

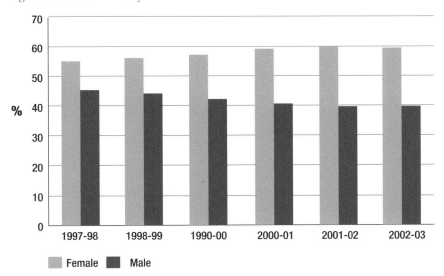

Figure 5.2 Gender breakdown first-year students. Source: HESA 1997-2003.

female, with the gap widening, as Figure 5.2 demonstrates. A look behind these cumulative data shows little progress in changing the proportion of men in nursing courses or women in engineering. Interestingly the gender divide among students from minority ethnic groups shows the same trend but a bigger gap, as Figure 5.3 demonstrates.

As student numbers continue to grow the planning system across the sector continues to focus on full-time students, yet as Figure 5.4 shows the dominance of the full-time student is declining as part-time numbers grow.

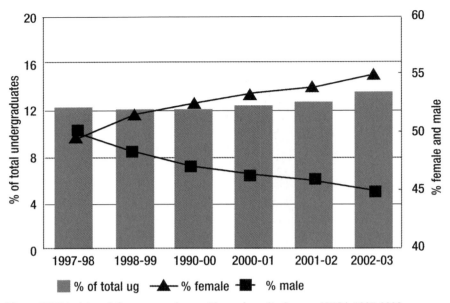

Figure 5.3 Ethnicity of first-year students with gender split. Source: HESA 1997-2003.

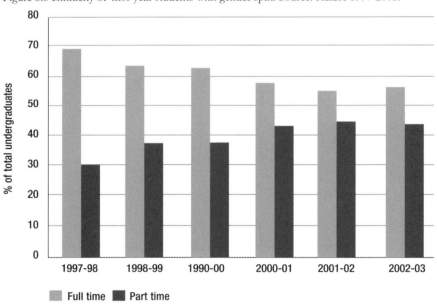

Figure 5.4 Full-time and part-time first-year students. Source: HESA 1997-2003.

Overall in UK higher education part-time students now represent 42 per cent of the student population (Higher Education Statistics Agency 2003) as shown in Figure 5.5. While the figures are not always easy to compare, given that many part-time students are studying at a much smaller scale, they still represent a large part of the HE community. The impact they have on an institution varies considerably, taking account of subject coverage, transport and local population.

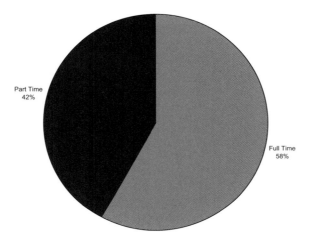

Figure 5.5 Students in higher education institutions 2001/02. Source: HESA 2003.

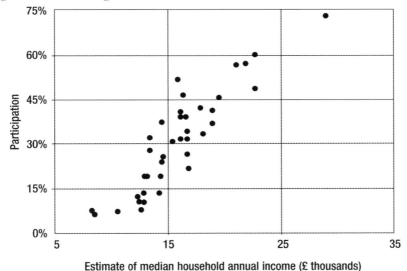

Figure 5.6 Participation in HE and family circumstances. Source: HEFCE 2001 (unpublished).

Of course the make-up of the student population continues to be dominated by those who can pay. Figure 5.6 shows how family income has a bearing on who is likely to study on a full-time basis.

The extent to which adult learners (over 21) participate in higher education is quite revealing. The major growth in UK higher education has been in part-time students. Of that, postgraduate study is the rapidly emerging area.

While no-one doubts the difficulty facing a number of adult learners, we should not assume that everyone is in that category. Some part-time postgraduate learners for example are very well supported in their study. The data that Ramsden's study (2004) revealed is where mature students are studying, and the extent to which part-time education is becoming segmented between the initial and recurrent.

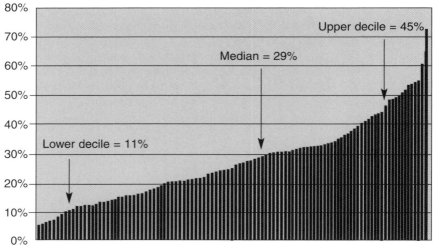

Figure 5.7 Percentage of mature full-time undergraduates 2001/02. Source: Ramsden 2004.

Figure 5.7 is taken from Ramsden (2004). It shows how mature full-time students are distributed across universities and colleges. A similar chart for minority ethnic group participation shows a polarised sector.

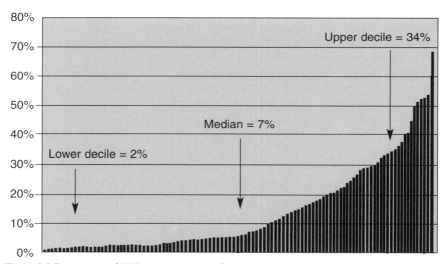

Figure 5.8 Percentage of UK entrants coming from ethnic minority groups, 2001/02. Source: Ramsden 2004.

This exclusive focus on full time means that the policy drive is celebrating achievement out of context with need. For example the much heralded Sutton Trust research demonstrates that more state school pupils now attend the leading universities. It moves on to equate attendance at state school to be coterminous with being disadvantaged, does not take account of state selective education, and does not provide a cash benefit analysis for the additional government funding that went to those universities to secure this change. £18 million over three years went to a small group of universities to help young people who were already more than likely going to one university to go to a different one, simply moving the deckchairs around. This works out at about £3,000 per student as a unit of resource to go to a different higher education institution. With £3,000 per student extra funding for adults we could make real inroads into social inclusion.

Sector dichotomy

The analysis we have of the sector recognises its diversity and different models of attendance. The planning and policy drive though is virtually exclusively based on sequential progression from school to university. Much is often talked of the need to look at work-related study as an entry route, but little is done.

We often talk of higher education as if it is a homogenous activity and as if we all have an understanding of what it is. We may have different views, but there will be some common ground. However, if we look at what has happened in the education sector over the last few years we see that there is a need to continue to push coherent planning or joined-up thinking. The Government is undoubtedly committed to education, but it isn't sure what it wants to focus resources on most. Is it in pre-schools, or secondary or HE? It knows it has to spend but how and where? One of its first initiatives was to establish the Excellence in Cities programme which targeted resource at schools in the most deprived urban areas, to the exclusion of rural depriva-tion. This was a way of boosting the spending on schools in the inner city without needing to raise the unit of resource elsewhere as part of a national uplift and still staying within the original conservative spending limits. The allocation of Excellence Challenge funding shown in figure 5.9 demonstrates the urban focus of the initiative.

The concepts behind *The Learning Age* (Department for Education and Employment 1998) are still part of the bedrock of where many want the sector to be taken, but there is little evidence of the journey actually going in that direction. The commitment to moving towards 50 per cent of the 18–30-year-olds participating in HE is a non-negotiable part of life. We can make all sorts of 'angry of the Ivory Tower' and 'outraged of Sleepy Suburbs' comments until the cows come home but if we want to achieve anything we need to manage the hand we have been dealt. There are very positive ways of doing this. It really just means thinking creatively and out of the box.

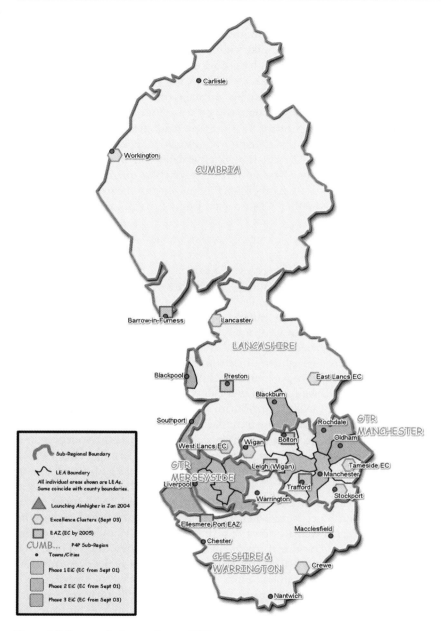

Figure 5.9. Source: Action on Access 2003.

Let us take the case study of the National Health Service. We know that doctors, dentists, optometrists, professions allied to medicine, etc. have really good licence to practise training, and we know about the registration and training process for nurses. However, they are only part of the workforce – what about all the other frontline services that look after us? What sort of training and development opportunities are available to them? How do we approach this? The moment that the Health Authority says they have a training need providers turn up like vultures at the door offering a quick fix and promising the earth or more. It is the dog-eat-dog nature of competition and survival. But what can we do?

The answer may be found in Newby's concept of lifelong learning which is in danger of being captured by some to be the saviour of the 14–19 agenda, rather than a real lifelong concept. Lifelong learning networks (LLNs) are not really about progression from a further education college (FEC) to a higher education institution (HEI). All that does is take you into a world where progression from one level to another is what the planning framework stipulates, and sorts out arrangements between the Learning and Skills Council (LSC) and Higher Education Funding Council for England (HEFCE). The real challenge for LLNs is to move towards the skills agenda, which is about people and economic planning, not simply about how to expand an HEI or a FEC.

The LLN is a radically different concept from that traditionally peddled as *tertiary*. The latter is most commonly vested in the notions of institutions providing in a different way to meet a variety of needs. The driving force becomes what the institution can do to meet needs within an economic imperative. The LLN in its ideal form is simply a system within which an individual can move around. The LLN therefore is an enabling/facilitating mechanism, whereas tertiary institutions are provider-centric. The difference is about demand-led and partnership compared to being supply-led and provider-managed. However, even in ideal worlds most partnerships contain an element of institutional protectionism.

Much of the debate about tertiary focuses on the role and nature of a further education college. That in itself poses a difficulty as the college sector is extraordinarily diverse. That sector faces a number of key challenges which will pose real issues concerning further engagement with the concept of tertiary.

The LSC is engaged in a process of retrenchment and it will focus on its core business over the coming years. This coupled with the direction coming out of the Strategic Area Reviews (STARs) in each LSC Area negates the likelihood that FE will be able to focus on tertiary as being F/HE. The STAR is a planning mechanism for an area to determine what is needed to fill the skills and educational attainment gaps. Arising from most such reviews is a planning requirement for colleges to focus on Basic Skills provision, level-2 programmes and the Increased Flexibility Programme. This is not a focus which reflects expansion of level 3 or expanding the role of HE in FE. There is a view that colleges are involved in mission stretch, which means that they are in danger of not being able to fulfil the core mission of meeting LSC objectives because their college focus is overly broad.

A large number of further education colleges have developed a range of higher education provision (Parry 2005). There are many and varied reasons for this, including government policy in respect of the development of

Foundation Degrees. However, the general pattern of such provision is one of declining enrolments and difficulty in meeting targets.

The challenge for lifelong learning networks as the enabler of tertiary

It is evident from all that has gone before that in order to address the issues facing participation from those currently under-represented in higher education we need a radically different planning base. Fiddling around on the margins will not deliver this. The key is not about the delivery of HE in FE. That is a relatively small but important part of the agenda. What is needed is a major programme of expansion at level 2, supported by further expansion at level 3, with progression routes into HE.

But if it is simply about the existing curriculum offering and cultural attitudes in HE then it could be argued that there is little point. It is time for HEIs actually to commit positively to a new form of widening participation, and develop the new routes through its curriculum.

The Aimhigher programme and its predecessors before that have set the agenda for progression into HE from and for the routes that exist today. The students from such schemes will be predominantly accessing traditional courses of study. The challenge for HE providers is to develop the new provision that will attract different learners. A comparison with an industrial process as shown in Figure 5.10 demonstrates that sometimes you need to change your process as a result of changing circumstances. To achieve this we need three key factors:

- A credit framework that transcends FE/HE;
- Expansion in FE;
- An understanding of different forms of HE.

This could be achieved geographically but could be mirrored at workforce sector level utilising the *Skills for the 21st Century* White Paper. The workforce sector level could for example be based on the needs of a particular sector and the mapping of a framework across the country. An example, returning to the NHS, would be establishing a curriculum framework for the non-clinical, medical and nursing staff which provided progression and routes for staff in particular posts. This would be a model, which actually was based on workforce development, and would be demand-led rather than hoped for. All HEIs and FECs could be partners. All they would have to do would be to agree to enable movement through the agreed framework rather than having separate individual institutional schemes. This would be truly tertiary as it shifts away from provider territory into an enabling mechanism.

In conclusion, an approach that seeks to develop tertiary as a means of thinking and planning may well be ahead of its time, but it raises the issues of how we plan and take aspects forward. Perhaps the problem is not with the

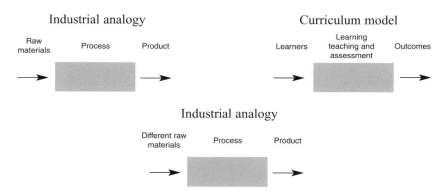

Figure 5.10 Collaboration over progression and the establishment of progression accords

idea and the concept but with some of the language. If *tertiary* is simply a planning model to take forward mechanisms to be able to deliver a more integrated approach then that is progress. It will be retrograde if it begins as a view from higher education and is seen as another initiative from one sector trying to shape what happens in another sector. The radical potential of *tertiary* is to plan higher education on the basis of what is needed to satisfy demand, taking account of economic and social policy strategies. But will universities buy that?

References

Action on Access (2003) *Aimhigher Integration*, 05/2003. Bradford: University of Bradford.

Department for Education and Employment (DfEE) (1998) *The Learning Age: A Renaissance for a New Britain*, Cm. 3790. London: HMSO.

Department for Education and Employment (DfEE) (2000) *The Excellence Challenge*. London: HMSO.

Higher Education Funding Council for England (2004) *Lifelong Learning Networks*, 12/2004 (June). Bristol: HEFCE.

Higher Education Funding Council for England (2004) *Aimhigher: Guidance Notes for Integration*, 08/2004 (LSC circular 04/01). Bristol: HEFCE.

Higher Education Statistics Agency (1997 to 2003) *Students in Higher Education Institutions*. Cheltenham: HESA.

Learning and Skills Council (2003) *Strategic Area Reviews*. Coventry: LSC.

NIACE *Adult Learning at a Glance*. Leicester: NIACE.

Parry, Gareth (2005) in G. Layer (ed.), *Closing the Equity Gap*. Leicester: NIACE

Ramsden, Brian (2004) *Patterns of Higher Education Institutions in the UK*, Fourth Report. London: Universities UK.

Issues and examples

CHAPTER SIX

The building of a dual-sector university: The Case of Thames Valley University[1]

Neil Garrod

Introduction

The merger of Thames Valley University with Reading College and School of Arts & Design on 1 January 2004 represented a significant and important milestone in the development of post-16 provision in the Thames Valley and nationally.

The resultant university is a genuinely dual-sector or tertiary education institution, with equal commitment given to both higher and further education, and a mission to encourage and enable progression within and between them. The current balance between higher and further education is 70:30 and there are no plans to change this balance in the short to medium term (5 years). While other universities have pockets of further education activity none have such a high proportion. The University of the Arts, London, formerly the London Institute, has a proportion of further education provision that approaches that of Thames Valley, but the lion's share of their further education provision is students on foundation course for their own higher education awards. At Thames Valley the further education provision operates across the full range of further education activity.

With over 45,000 student registrations it is one of the largest institutions in the higher education sector in the UK. Its diversity is reflected not just in the range of subjects it offers – from accounting and finance to video production – and in the levels of provision – from further education access courses through to doctoral research work – that are offered, but also in its rich and complex student profile – over 126 nationalities, 45 per cent ethnic minorities, 60 per cent female, 60 per cent part-time students and 50 per cent over the age of 30.

What sectors are we in?

The concept of operating the full range of post-compulsory education within a single institution is an unfamiliar one in the UK and there is no currently recognised name that encapsulates the full ambit of further and higher education. Tertiary is one title that is growing in currency. Indeed, the term was used in the Strategic Plan of Thames Valley University that was sent to HEFCE in July of 2004.

However, things move on quickly at Thames Valley and four months later and eleven months into the merger we are using the term dual-sector to identify the environment in which we operate. The duality reflects the operational and financial differences between further and higher education in the UK.

In reality Thames Valley University is a triple sector university, with around 20 per cent of its teaching funding coming from the National Health Service (NHS), a further 20 per cent from the Learning and Skills Council (LSC) and the remainder from the Higher Education Funding Council for England (HEFCE). However, the meshing of the NHS and HEFCE systems is an old story and largely resolved. The reason for emphasising now that the university operates in a dual sector is due to the significant differences that exist between the two educational sectors, further and higher, that the university spans and that create significant internal organisational pressures that need to be managed.

How is the duality manifest?

While there may be differences between further and higher education emanating from the age profile of students, their previous educational background, the staff that teach them and the employment contracts within which those staff operate, the greatest duality emanates from the distinct sources of funding of the two sectors and the associated philosophies and modes of operation that are linked to them. Historically this was reflected in the local/national government funding differentiation between the sectors that was further complicated by the 1988 Education Reform Act and then rationalised under the Further and Higher Education Act 1992.

Despite certain remaining idiosyncrasies between the two funding schemes[2] the most pressing current divergence emanates from the future development plans of the respective funding bodies. The move towards top-up fees with a specific government commitment to the maintenance of the unit of resource[3] for higher education means that universities will have increasing discretion over their own funding levels through their fee structures. The proposals from the Conservative Party, including funded student numbers following demand rather than HEFCE approved admission targets, will only extend the concept of a market-based system where funding is increasingly in the hands of the universities.[4]

On the other hand the latest funding proposal from LSC is entitled 'Plan-Led Funding for Further Education'.[5] Under the proposal funding is to become more focused on particular groups of learners[6] that, in turn, will reduce the funding available to other groups. To meet this decline 'implies developing new ways of increasing fee income and contributions from learners and employers'.[7] Thus the qualification offer will be increasingly directed and fee income is seen as a replacement, rather than an additional, source of funding. Our experience suggests that the gulf between the two funding schemes is widening rather than narrowing.[8]

From where does the duality arise?

The distinction between higher and further education appears to be a UK, or Commonwealth, construct largely absent from continental Europe and the United States of America. The genesis of any such distinction is somewhat murky and the concept of further education tends to emerge as a residual, once higher education has been defined and removed from the post-compulsory education panoply.

For example, the Robbins Report on Higher Education (Committee on Higher Education 1963) defines universities as 'institutions in receipt of Treasury grant'[9] while further education 'comprises all other institutions providing post-school education (other than adult education) within the sphere of responsibility of the Minister of Education or the Secretary of State for Scotland'.

By the time of Dearing (National Committee of Enquiry into Higher Education 1997) the wording is a little more detailed and does refer to educational as well as institutional differences. Higher education is 'educational provision above level 3 (i.e. above A level and Advanced level GNVQ) and its equivalents in Scotland' while further education is 'provision for people over compulsory school age which does not take place in a secondary school and which falls within the scope of Schedule 2 to the Further and Higher Education Act 1992'.[10] However, no clear rationale for sourcing further and higher education in different institutions is provided, other than the source of funding itself. Indeed the concept of offering both further and higher education in the same institution is casually supported by Dearing in his Annexe E glossary definition of further education that ends with the sentence 'further education may take place in sixth form colleges, further education colleges or higher education institutions'[7]. When one considers that roughly 10 per cent of higher education courses are offered through further education colleges then the concept of tertiary education begins to take real shape. The focus of this chapter on duality is to underscore the unfortunate and consequential impact of separate funding routes and philosophies that currently exist between higher and further education.

While Dearing explicitly limited its remit to higher rather than tertiary education for largely pragmatic reasons,[11] the committee did consider a single funding council for further and higher education. However, a case was made strongly against such a proposal by HEFCE on the general grounds of size and complexity that specifically argued that 'despite overlap and synergy, the further and higher education sectors remained largely distinct in institutional and academic terms'; that 'a blurring of the sectors may lead to an upward mission drift by FE colleges';[12] and with a 'concern over management stretch'.[13]

While no support was forthcoming on a single funding agency from Dearing, neither was there clarity on their preferred option. In England and Wales higher education would be funded by the respective higher education funding bodies, wherever that provision was offered. On the other hand Scotland and Northern Ireland were allowed to continue with their own preferred option of limiting higher education funding to degree level and above (i.e. provision that was only offered by universities) and that all sub-degree qualifications would be funded by the further education funding body.

Variety (confusion) abounds as to what exactly is meant by further and higher education and, therefore, Thames Valley University is a dual-sector institution because of the duality of the funding regimes that apply to the portfolio of learning opportunities that it offers. Whether there is a clear educational, pedagogical or philosophical distinction is an outstanding issue, not too dissimilar to that of the 'honours challenge'. The identification of any such differences will feed not only into curriculum design and related pedagogy but also into issues relating to quality audit and management, and differences in contracts of employment between academic staff involved in teaching and learning at the different levels. Increasingly Thames Valley is coming up against practical issues that would be informed by increased clarity on the distinctions and/or similarities between further and higher education from an educational, pedagogical and philosophical standpoint.

The case for merger

The former Thames Valley University and Reading College and School of Arts & Design had been close collaborators since 1999, with franchise programmes running at the Reading College site in computing, multimedia and music from September 2000.

For both institutions this relationship formed only a part of their respective portfolios of partnerships. Thames Valley University had worked with West London colleges, such as Hammersmith West London & Ealing College, and Kingston College. Reading College had partnership arrangements with higher education institutes to provide local progression opportunities for their further education students, specifically with the University of Lincoln, the University of Reading, Oxford Brookes University, and Buckinghamshire Chiltern University College. However, it was the conclusion of both institutions that these evolving and complex arrangements had been unable to support and sustain a stable and coherent planning framework, and were considered to have hindered the overall development of clear progression pathways from further to higher education. It was this desire to develop clearer and more successful progression pathways that was the driving concept behind the merger.

At first blush the conclusion to merge might be seen as direct questioning of the conclusion drawn by HEFCE and the Dearing Committee[14] that a full tertiary model was inappropriate across the sector. On the contrary Thames Valley University would not dispute this conclusion. It is important to clarify that the two former institutions considered merger appropriate in their particular circumstances but the new Thames Valley is not, necessarily, an advocate of mergers across the sector. It is agnostic about the suitability of mergers. Rather, the University believes that much can be learned about the potential costs and benefits of such structural change by studying its own journey. However, it is worth recognising at the outset that Thames Valley is faced with a more challenging and, even, hostile environment in the absence of a truly tertiary system. Sector differences need to be internalised and dealt with in a way that does not impact upon single-sector institutions to the same extent.

Post-merger developments

Improved progression opportunities for students had been identified in the Case for Merger as the primary rationale for merger: '. . . over the past 5 years a number of FE:HE relationships have developed in the Thames valley region . . . these . . . have been unable to support . . . a stable and coherent planning framework and . . . clear progression pathways'. This established a clear metric against which success of the merger and the University could be measured, as well as a dominant framework within which post-merger mission could be developed and organisational change take place.

Fortunately/coincidentally/unfortunately Thames Valley was due to submit a new strategic plan to HEFCE in mid-2004, just six months following the merger. In retrospect this helped rather than hindered the process. The primary issue that faced the post-merger institution was the development of an identity and organisational structure but the need to submit a strategic plan ensured that such structures were developed with a strategic focus, were clearly documented, and linked to operational issues and performance measures. Whether such a clear articulation of post-merger structures and aspirations would have emerged in the absence of the strategic plan deadlines is, in my view, questionable. Suffice it to say that by the end of January it was clear that the internal organisational restructuring issues and long-term strategy were inextricably linked and, effectively, considered jointly.

A strategic planning awayday was held on 1 March at which members of the Core Executive of the former Thames Valley University and the Senior Management Team of the former Reading College and School of Arts & Design were present. Presentations were made by the PVC/Deans of the former TVU faculties, the Director of Reading Campus (formerly the Deputy Principal of Reading College and School of Arts & Design and to be redesignated, in August 2004, Director of Further Education) and support service heads. In summarising the presentations and subsequent discussions the Deputy Vice-Chancellor identified five major themes common to the presentations that within the space of about a week had become the new mission equivalent. To paraphrase the strategic plan:

To encapsulate the aspirations and modes of operation of a dual-sector institution with progression at the heart of its mission within a single statement is a daunting task. Rather we prefer to rely on a series of value propositions that locate the University, encapsulate its aspirations, and reveal the parameters within which these aspirations are to be realised.

We champion and support five such value propositions.

1. We are a university

The role of a university, *inter alia*, is to widen horizons and challenge existing paradigms. Thames Valley will pursue these goals in their more traditional sense with a special focus on widening the horizons of its students and raising their own confidence to achieve their full potential.

The title of the University underscores its commitment to the region within which its campuses are located while reaffirming its responsibility, as a university, to the wider academic and international community. This dual focus also reflects the international nature of London and the Thames Valley itself.

2. Growth through full participation

A proposition that is being tested by the very establishment of the University is that the profile of those that can benefit from a university education is wider than previous practice would suggest.

Full participation means the attraction and involvement of all students who can benefit from and contribute to a university education, including those who, historically, would never have participated in tertiary education. To break into this circle of social underachievement is a major aspiration of the University. The further education offerings of the University provide a special focus on craft and skills training, but as a university it is incumbent upon us to go beyond skills and vocational training. Just as with the great professions and original vocational qualifications in law, medicine and theology, we are committed to the development of educational pathways that provide vocational direction while also introducing students to the wider schema offered through more broad-based learning and knowledge. Our students deserve to be empowered in a world of ideas.

3. Curricula and qualifications in support of full participation

The single most striking opportunity offered by the merger is the development of a qualification framework that facilitates and encourages progression across the full range of tertiary education. This must be reflected within any newly adopted academic structure of the University.

The changing nature of the workplace and vocational drivers requires that we constantly monitor opportunities for creative developments, within and across subject areas, within and across further/higher education boundaries, within and across undergraduate/postgraduate boundaries, and within and across our regional business partners.

4. Full participation for staff as well as students

Full participation at a student level requires the simultaneous development of staff to take advantage of new demands from the growing and changing student body. At the very minimum, greater numbers of academic staff will be required to deal with the growth of student numbers, even within a regime of a falling unit of resource. Perhaps more pertinently, the changing student profile, resulting from success in achieving full participation, must lead to a reassessment of the skills required by academic staff and the nature of their academic practice. The University will create a structured framework of staff development within which existing staff can enhance their own capabilities and contributions to the aspirations of the University, existing students will aspire to become future academic staff and those who wish to change the nature of their contribution to the student body and the University are empowered so to do.

Research underpins the basic university aspirations of widening horizons and challenging existing paradigms. In a university that is committed to full participation and the empowerment of its students within a world of ideas they are critical. The University, through its newly formed Research Office, will encourage and celebrate research as fundamental. Staff will be supported in their research aspirations. For experienced researchers in their field there will be enhanced support for the resources and environment in which their work can flourish; for those with less or no research background a structured and supportive environment will be created that allows them to develop their research skills, enhance their scholarship profile and develop into research leaders.

5. Releasing potential through budgetary processes

Budget design is critical to the release of the creative potential that resides within the University. The University will develop its budgetary system so that it rewards success and provides guidance for increased efficiency in the achievement of its core aspirations. The creative potential of the academic and support staff to develop new programmes, new curricular mixes, new pedagogical mixes and more efficient methods of operation are all encouraged by a motivational budget as well as being informed by a clear indication of their financial implications.

Such a budgetary model will facilitate the embedding of commercial and third-stream income-generation processes within the daily activities of the University.

Knowledge is transferred from the education sector into the wider world through the skills and experience gained by its graduates. It is also transferred through funded and unfunded research, through consultancy, through interactions with business and the public services, and through work with schools and the community. An open and transparent budgetary system recognises these alternatives and enables an informed evaluation of the most appropriate mix of the mechanisms available, in order to maximise the impact of the University on society.[15]

Academic structure of the University

Any merged institution needs to review its administrative and operational structures. The value propositions provided a framework within which academic structures could be critically reviewed. Four issues were considered fundamental to the review of existing academic structures and the design of any new academic structure:

- to underscore the aspirations of the University to facilitate progress throughout the expanded range of offerings at sixth form, further education, undergraduate and postgraduate levels;
- to reaffirm the role and importance of scholarship and knowledge transfer in the University's endeavours;
- to allow flexibility within the academic structure to enable suitable responses to emerging demands;
- to facilitate communication between equivalent positions within the University.

The academic structures of the former constituent institutions were very similar. The former Thames Valley University operated with three faculties: Health and Human Sciences, Professional Studies and the London College of Music and Media. Reading College and School of Arts & Design operated with five faculties, one being Enterprise whose primary role was the coordination, and in some cases delivery, of a range of programmes that ran across the other faculties. Examples would be contract coordination of work-based learning contracts, employer training contracts and community-based learning. The other faculties were: Business and Service Industries, Technology, Education and Care and the Berkshire School of Arts and Design.

Apart from technology, there was considerable overlap between the subject portfolios of the two former institutions, and the academic units had the same span of duties, namely subject and curriculum development. However, their focus was different, as reflected in the titles of the academic leaders below the level of the Dean or Head of Faculty: curriculum manager and subject area head. The importance of maintaining and developing a coherent set of curriculum and qualification offerings that attract high levels of demand, while at the same time bolstering staff development, general levels of scholarship and the reputation of subject areas, suggested a new structure that recognised explicitly these two responsibilities. Such recognition would enable a clear focus to be developed for those that lead in these areas of focus, and for success to be clearly monitored.

Two distinct dimensions were thereby identified: one that focuses on staff and subject development and one that focuses on curriculum and qualification development. The heads of the units on each of these dimensions would be jointly responsible for the design of academic offerings and developments.

In the November of 2003, just preceding merger, Reading College and School of Arts & Design had failed an Office for Standards in Education (Ofsted) inspection. This meant that a re-inspection was timetabled for November 2005. In addition Thames Valley University was scheduled for a Quality Assurance Agency (QAA) Institutional Audit at the same time. Both events meant that immediate movement to any new structure would be problematic. However, at a series of meetings chaired by the Deputy Vice-Chancellor between the PVC/Deans of the faculties of former Thames Valley University and the Heads of the four academic faculties of Reading College and School of Arts & Design, along with the Director of Reading Campus (formerly Vice-Principal of Reading College and School of Arts & Design to be redesignated Director of Further Education in August 2004) held during February and March, the following structure was agreed.

This structure embodies the two distinct roles identified above. Directors of studies for curriculum clusters lead on curriculum and qualification development, and have roles crossing subject areas. Heads of subject area have responsibilities for staff and subject development and have roles extending from taught postgraduate work through undergraduate work to further education.

The Sixth Form Academy and the Graduate School lie outside this formal structure. The Sixth Form Academy had existed as a separate operational unit within Reading College and School of Arts & Design and had demonstrated the success of internally differentiated units when the target market is quite distinct.[16] While the Sixth Form College would retain its own staff they would be encouraged to join the relevant faculty-based subject areas and be considered a University resource. The Graduate School is a new development. While leaving academic programmes within the subject areas and faculties, the Graduate School is conceived to provide a focus and additional support for postgraduate students and staff teaching on postgraduate programmes, as well as coordinating teaching and learning programmes and research training.

The proposed structure was adopted by Academic Board in April 2004 and endorsed by the Board of Governors in May 2004. The parameters of the academic structure are now firmly set: the building blocks of the academic offer of the University will be developed around subject groups that are further clustered within faculties; those subject groups will contain the full range of offer of the University within that subject area, from access to further education to doctoral work; and the strategic and operational aspects of the offer will be the joint responsibility of Heads of Subject and Directors of Study within plans set by faculties and approved by Faculty Boards. As well as highlighting the importance of the comprehensive programme portfolio that reflects the duality of the University and the importance of the development of staff and academic integrity and reputation within subject areas, the revised structure creates a group of academic leaders or manager academics that have identifiable equivalents throughout the University and who are, collectively, responsible for academic policy and standards.

Progress towards the new structure

In designing the new structure considerable emphasis was placed on the need for stability due to the anticipated Ofsted re-inspection of further education provision on the Reading campus as well as the QAA's Institutional Audit of the University, both in 2005. Following the adoption of the new academic structure the University learned that a full re-inspection of the further education provision on the Reading campus would now not take place. Ofsted had recognised that a re-inspection of only a part of the further education provision of Thames Valley University made no practical or pedagogical sense. Rather, individual curriculum areas would be monitored for progress to a satisfactory appraisal. While the momentum to improvement built up through the implementation of the Action Plan needs to be maintained, the focus on individual curriculum areas meant that this can be achieved within any structure that maintains the integrity of the further education provision within specific curriculum areas on the Reading campus.

    This allowed progress towards the new academic structure to be much speedier than at first envisaged. Interviews for all Heads of Subject and Directors of Study roles were completed by the middle of November 2004. Speed of progress towards full integration of all further and higher education within the faculties varies across faculties and subject groups but was planned to be completed throughout the University by Easter 2005.

    It was considered important from the outset that any revised academic structure must allow for internal faculty flexibility around the basic structure. Thus the Head of Faculty (Pro Vice-Chancellor/Dean), Heads of Subject and Directors of Study were the only positions defined on a university-wide basis. It is likely that faculties will feel it necessary to identify other roles. This is left to faculties so that their own internal structures can reflect their own specific environment and circumstances. This flexibility is further reflected in the diversity of approach to the areas of responsibility of the Directors of Study. In some areas they are level-based (further education, undergraduate, post-graduate), in some they are subject-based, and some are a mixture.

The merger brought a new area of academic endeavour to the University, namely Technology. This subject area encapsulates engineering and construction. It is anticipated that the Technology subject group will become a faculty of the University in due course. However, the balance of further and higher education in this subject group is overwhelmingly further education, currently around 85 per cent further education (levels 1–3) and 15 per cent higher education (levels 4–6). In line with the aspiration of the University to develop a portfolio of offerings that span the full range of tertiary education it is not felt appropriate, at this stage, to grant faculty title. However, it is an aspiration of the University that this area of academic endeavour be supported to develop into a faculty. Linked to the expansion of higher education courses and the development of graduate and postgraduate provision will be an associated increased focus on research and scholarship in this area.

The final academic structure is, therefore, as in Figure 6.1.

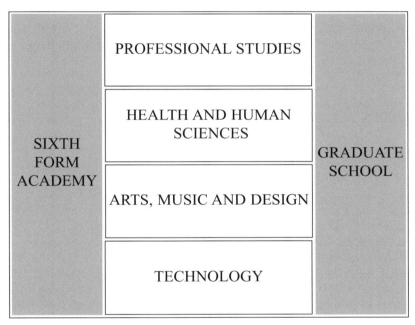

Figure 6.1

Additional aspects of the academic structure

Further education

The movement to a full dual-sector institution by extending the range of further education work within the University will necessarily place specific and, often, new challenges on the faculties. To support this transition and enable movement to a full and comprehensive qualifications portfolio as quickly as possible a support structure for faculties and their further education work was established. A Director of Further Education was appointed to coordinate the harmonisation of further education systems and processes, coordinate relationships with the further education funding bodies, advise faculties on their own specific further education offerings, offer guidance on the strategic development of further education and a balanced qualification portfolio, and generally support the establishment of further education as an important and integral part of faculty operations.

The Director of Further Education will work with and draw on the resources of current academic resource groupings such as quality audit, academic office and teaching and learning. Each of these areas is developing its own post-merger structures, and these developments will inform the structure of further education support.

Research and scholarship

A robust culture of research and scholarship is fundamental to the university's strategic objectives. It enables achievement in scholarship and research in key areas of expertise. It is also central to the university's academic and professional character, supporting aspirations for the highest standards in teaching and learning for all students. Curricula that are underpinned by research ensure that students have the opportunity to be taught by scholars and practitioners who are at the forefront of developments in their disciplines.

Research is coordinated and monitored through the recently established Research Office with a view to developing a research culture that spans the full tertiary spectrum of Thames Valley University. This is encapsulated in the adoption of Ernest Boyer's well established scholarship categories of 'discovery', 'application', integration' and 'teaching'. The strategy combines research in many different subjects, including educational pedagogy, to underpin the University's commitment to the transfer of knowledge and the provision of a world-class education to students from all.

Effecting the widening participation agenda in its widest social context is central to the aspirations of the University. Strong and active links with business, research-based institutions, colleges and universities as well as the teaching and learning strategy itself all contribute to this goal. These aspirations mean that Thames Valley will be at the forefront of change in educational policy and pedagogy, and also a live laboratory for such change. In recognition of this, the University has established an educational policy and pedagogical research group, led by the Head of Educational Development in collaboration with recognised experts from sister institutions. Research into our innovative approaches to student-centred learning, work-based learning, widening participation and student retention will form a major thrust of research to which all academic staff can contribute.

The new academic structure underscores the full tertiary education spectrum over which the University operates. Progression is a central institutional goal and sets one significant quantum against which the success and value of the merger can be established. With over 6,000 level-3 students within the University, including some 1,200 A-level students within the Sixth

Form College, the establishment of a programmes portfolio that highlights a clear and attractive articulation between level-3 and level-4 programmes and beyond is essential.

Whilst the level-3/level-4 progression point is a critical one, the University is keen to develop progression at all levels. The plan is to develop a qualification portfolio that addresses progression issues at level 3/level 4, level 6/level 7 and level 7/level 8. This will be done both internally and through collaboration and external networks. In this regard Thames Valley will play a leading role in lifelong learning networks. Existing links both with further education colleges throughout the region and with research-based institutions put the University in an ideal position to develop the LLN concept in a comprehensive fashion. The current link with Imperial College is an exemplar of how the University will act as a gateway to the very best research-led institutions for both students and staff.

Outstanding and emerging issues

The first nine months of the merged institution have been dynamic and exhilarating. My perception is no doubt heavily influenced by the fact that they coincided with my own first nine months at Thames Valley. Nonetheless the glow of pregnancy has passed and the crying baby is now in full voice. With the structures in place efforts are now directed towards the implementation of strategy and the measurement of success.

Issues that are emerging or taking on greater prominence following the rapid change during the early part of 2004 are:

1. The need for a comprehensive staff development programme that reflects the aspirations set out in the Strategic Plan and reflected in the revised academic structures.

While implicit within Value Proposition number 4, the support needed for staff to rise to the challenge of the merger and to take their own careers forward is constantly recurring. Pressure on time and resources means that an effective programme of staff development is critical. For the future this implies much greater collaboration between the more traditional programme of staff development opportunities, generally focused around skills and of very short duration, and the opportunity offered through the Graduate School for, potentially, credit-based learning and teaching, scholarship and service programmes.

2. Issues surrounding the nature of estates and resourcing integration or differentiation across the dual sectors.

Estates development is an increasing focus for universities as the unit of resource declines and the proportional value of the estate increases. Effective utilisation of the estate is of critical importance to health in the income and expenditure statement. Thames Valley faces all of these generic problems but as a dual-sector institution faces the additional thorny issue of whether and how different levels of programmes and students retain their own identity within the broader institution.

Naturally there is a spectrum of possible solutions ranging from complete separation (the senior and junior common room approach) through to the removal of any differentiation. For a newly merged dual-sector institution that has based its academic structure on facilitated progression across and between different educational levels the separation end of the spectrum looks particularly unattractive. However, there are those that advocate such a split and there is even the suggestion that students would welcome it. The argument is that 'college' students want to go 'away' to university if they progress into higher education. If this is a widely felt view among students then as a university that is profoundly concerned with progression it cannot be ignored simply on philosophical grounds.

We believe that the trick here is to eschew the simplifying assumptions of the solutions at either end of the spectrum. Resource limitations mean that the duplication of resources for the two sectors (ignoring similar issues when one considers undergraduate versus postgraduate, honours year versus other undergraduate years, doctoral versus masters, etc., etc.) are unlikely to be realistic; students are motivated by concepts of progression that bring tangible benefits in learning environment and resources; higher-level work will demand a richer portfolio of resources and more specific estates provision; assisting in the learning of others is very supportive of a student's own learning; aspirations are raised by the constructive mixing of students from different levels of study; a separation of students from the two sectors would not be helpful in raising the level of debate about the evolution of the concept of a university.

For all of the above reasons we believe that we have to develop creative solutions, and we recognise that there may be many, that create feelings of membership without establishing feelings of exclusion. We anticipate this largely to come from fostering concepts of multiple cultures within the university which will be very strongly enforced through creative estates strategies.

3. Are the 'cultural' differences between the two sectors real or imaginary?

The duality of the University that emanates from the funding differences between the two sectors has been emphasised. Experiences to date however all suggest that while there are particular nuances surrounding pedagogy and quality in the two sectors there is an increasing sense of a generic framework existing upon which those nuances can be overlaid. This is considered to be a research thrust of particular importance to the University and will form core business for the newly created research institute at Thames Valley, the Centre for Research in Tertiary Education (CREATE).

4. Are the complexities of trying to operate over a dual sector too difficult to be dealt with internally within a single institution?

Issues of:

- *pedagogical distinction*
- *concept of scholarship*: A thorny enough problem in simple higher education institutions. In a dual-sector institution it is overlaid by increased layers of complexity and is, again, a debate that we wish to contribute to through a rigorous analysis of our own experiences.
- *contractual differences*: Personally I am very committed to the development of a single contract of employment for all academic staff within a dual-sector university. The difficulties and complexities mean that others involved in the process of negotiation are pushing for the more straightforward maintenance of two separate contracts: one for further education lecturers and one for higher education lecturers. If this is agreed I think it a very unfortunate missed opportunity in underscoring the aspiration and philosophy of the University.
- *management stretch*: Are the array of issues that face a dual-sector institution simply too great to be handled by anyone?

5. Will the Tomlinson Report help, hinder or be neutral to our success?

Irrespective of what happens to the Report following the proposed White Paper there are many proposals contained within the Report that mirror our own development and that we shall incorporate, particularly with regard to the programme portfolio and its internal linkages.

6. In the light of staff, as well as student, progression, how do we prevent mission drift?

This is a vitally important issue that is exacerbated by our focus on progression. We must avoid the concept, for both students and staff, that lack of progression is failure. Equally we need to raise aspirations. Ensuring one without the other will be a complex task.

Notes

1 In preparing this paper I have benefited considerably from discussions with Ron Barnett, David Melville and Bruce Macfarlane. I thank them for their generosity of time and recognise the impact of their insights into my own perceptions and thinking.
2 See Parry and Thompson, *Closer by Degrees* (2002), p. 6 for further details.
3 Secretary of State for Education and Skills, Charles Clarke, statement to the House of Commons regarding the Spending Review Settlement.

4   http://www.conservatives.com/
    tile.do?def=news.story.page&obj_id=116628
5   Learning and Skills Council Circular 04/02.
6   The currently identified priority groups are the low-skilled, 16–18 age
    group and those without level-2 qualifications.
7   Learning and Skills Council Circular 03/02, para. 53.
8   It is worth musing on the potential impact of these divergent policies on
    student demand and supply. On the supply side there could be a
    significant growth in higher education numbers and restriction on
    further education numbers outside of the identified priority areas. If this
    occurs it is difficult to see from whence the equivalent demand will be
    generated that will lead to any sort of equilibrium. Interestingly this
    possibility is quite the reverse of the situation that occurred in the early
    1990s that led to the expansion of franchises of higher education in
    further education institutions.
9   p. 317.
10 Dearing Report, 1997 Annexe E.
11 Some consider this to be a weakness of the report as it created
    difficulties when proposals were made that impacted on other sectors,
    see e.g. Parry 1999, pp. 225–41.
12 As had previously happened with the Polytechnic sector, particularly
    following the abolition of the binary divide, see e.g. Pratt 1997.
13 HEFCE 1997.
14 No view had ever been expressed by FEFC to Dearing on a single
    funding body.
15 Thames   Valley   University   2004,   http://www.tvu.ac.uk/theuni/
    1policy_docs/strategic_plan.doc
16 Apart from A level studies The Sixth Form Academy offered access
    courses, foundation courses, courses for students with learning disabili-
    ties and a full range of 14–19 provision.

References

Committee on Higher Education (1963) *Higher Education Report of the
    Committee appointed by the Prime Minister under the Chairmanship of Lord Robbins
    1961–1963*. London: HMSO.
Higher Education Funding Council for England (1997) *Submission to the
    National Committee of Inquiry into Higher Education*. Bristol: HEFCE.
Learning and Skills Council (2004) *Plan-Led Funding for Further Education*,
    Circular 04/02. Coventry: LSC.
National Committee of Enquiry into Higher Education (1997) *Higher
    Education in the Learning Society*, Report of the National Committee of
    Inquiry into Higher Education, chaired by Sir Ron (now Lord) Dearing,
    House of Lords Papers, 1997–98. London: The Stationery Office.

Parry, G. (1999) 'Education research and policy making in higher education: the case of Dearing', *Journal of Education Policy* 14.3, pp. 225–41.

Parry G. and A. Thompson (2002) *Closer by Degrees*. London: Learning and Skills Development Agency (LSDA).

Pratt, J. (1997) *The Polytechnic Experiment 1965–1992*. Milton Keynes: Open University Press.

Thames Valley University (2004) *Strategic Plan: 2004 and Beyond*. London: Thames Valley University. Available online at http://www.tvu.ac.uk/theuni/1policy_docs/strategic_plan.doc.

CHAPTER SEVEN

A view from the sideline: The role of access to higher education courses in relation to lifelong learning networks

Kath Dentith

Introduction

We have, as Sir Howard Newby remarked in his Colin Bell Memorial Lecture, 'been here before'. In introducing his vision of lifelong learning networks, Newby sketched progress made in widening access since the late 1960s, including the remit from the Council for National Academic Awards (CNAA) to extend access to a wider range of students, and the subsequent development of access courses and other initiatives which 'significantly advanced the cause of widening participation long before it became a political imperative' (see Newby 2005). Some of those initiatives have, of course, since been superseded by other developments, but some, including Access to Higher Education (HE), are still very much with us and continue to play a major role in advancing the cause of widening participation.

In the same lecture, Newby also noted the importance of having 'not only more collaboration, but more connectivity', proposing 'an extension of best practice in a more formalised form which runs with the grain of much existing local and regional thinking'. This 'connectivity' is obviously essential for the development of coherent and effective strategy, as well as being important in avoiding duplication of effort and wastage of resource. It is not necessarily the most exciting part of policy development, and involves the somewhat laborious tasks of evaluating what already exists against meaningful criteria; assessing the success and admitting the limitations of earlier work; and being prepared to learn lessons from the limitations and build on the successes. So before moving on, and in a spirit of 'connectivity', it may be worth considering the particular contribution to widening participation made by Access to HE currently; and the potential for articulation with other initiatives – and with lifelong learning networks in particular – in the future.

A little history

As access courses proliferated in the 1970s and early 1980s it was realised that what was proving successful at the local level would benefit from being developed more systematically and within a broader framework. At the same time it was recognised that it would benefit students if there were national recognition for these locally validated courses and for the qualification awarded to students who successfully completed them. This was reflected in the call in the 1987 White Paper, *Higher Education: Meeting the Challenge* for 'a comprehensive framework within which the availability of well devised access courses can be increased' (DfEE 1987, p. 10).

As a result, the Council for National Academic Awards (CNAA) and Committee of Vice-Chancellors and Principals (CVCP) jointly established the original framework for Access courses recognition. Responsibility for regulating the framework passed to the Higher Education Quality Council in 1992 and then, in 1997, to the Quality Assurance Agency (QAA). The model provided by the framework for Access courses recognition has remained essentially the same over that time, with a national body which is responsible for licensing and reviewing local consortia of HE and further education (FE) institutions. Those consortia, the authorised validating agencies (AVAs), in turn, develop, validate and quality assure the courses, and award nationally recognised Access certificates to individual students. It is a model which has proved to have many strengths and which, because of the longevity of the scheme, has been subject to review and refinement over time.

Recent developments

That process of continuing review and refinement has been given particular impetus in the last two years. A more recent White Paper, *The Future of Higher Education* (DfES 2003), stated the Government's commitment to 'ensure that there are good quality and accessible 'second-chance' routes into HE for those who missed out when they were younger', and made specific reference to Access to HE courses, acknowledging that they had provided a 'valuable entry route into higher education for many students'. This provided an encouraging indication that the contribution made by Access to widening participation was recognised, and the White Paper's request that QAA should 'come forward with proposals to modernise the criteria for Access courses' indicated an interest in developing this success further.

In response to this request in the White Paper, QAA undertook a research project on Access to HE during 2003–04. The project report concluded with seven recommendations. These covered a wide range of issues, including funding; marketing and promotion; continuing development and enhancement; the nature of the Access qualification; and consistency in the description of student achievement. All are important in developing Access to HE further, but the first, and perhaps most important, recommendation called for 'a national strategy to support the development of Access to HE provision . . . which recognises the particular contribution to widening participation made by Access to HE and its relationship to other widening participation initiatives' (QAA 2004a, p. 3).

This recommendation reflected widespread concern voiced by respondents in HE and elsewhere about the absence of connectivity in relation to Access to HE and its strategic context. It was suggested that this had resulted in an anomalous situation in which, as widening participation had taken an increasingly central position in HE policy development, Access to HE courses (the central purpose of which is about widening participation in higher education) seemed, perversely, to have no identified place within that policy or in relation to the HE-based initiatives adopted to achieve this objective.

In its response to the QAA report, the Department for Education and Skills (DfES) acknowledged that there was 'a need for a more strategic approach to the role and development of Access courses' (QAA 2004b). The response stated that the DfES would take this forward within the Joint Progression Strategy, and that 'we will encourage institutional partnerships under the new initiative of *lifelong learning networks* to consider actively the role that Access courses currently play in vocational progression to HE, and whether and how this might be developed further'. The relationship between the Access Recognition Scheme and lifelong learning networks could, therefore, be central to the future development of Access to HE, and Access courses could feature strongly in plans developed by lifelong learning networks. If lifelong learning networks, as a key mechanism for widening participation in higher education, are to be able to take advantage of the particular role played by Access courses, and develop that, it will be important that they have a clear view about the kinds of success Access has achieved, how that has been achieved, and where the greatest potential for further development lies.

A sense of proportion

In claiming that Access to HE plays 'a major role' in widening participation and suggesting its value to lifelong learning networks, we should be clear what evidence is available to support this claim. QAA has been looking at this question over the last five years. While we should be cautious about how we use the data from different sources together, certain things are now clear.

- There have been steady increases in the numbers passing successfully through Access courses and progressing into and through HE over the last five years.
- The number of courses has also increased, and there are now over 1,500 QAA-recognised Access to HE programmes in England and Wales.
- Over 400 providers are involved in the delivery of Access programmes, 86 per cent of them FE colleges.
- Of about 13,000 students entering HE with some kind of 'access' qualification in 2002, HESA reports that over 11,000 had an Access to HE certificate from a QAA-recognised Access course.
- The average age of Access students has gradually fallen, and about 50 per cent are now under 30.

Access students are particularly well represented in some specific vocational areas. Access students going on to study nursing in HE through the NMAS route, for example, make up 14 per cent of the total student intake.

The ethnicity profile of Access students shows that some of the most under-represented groups in HE are comparatively well represented among the Access population. For example, LSC data show that 13.5 per cent Access students are Black or Black British, compared with about 4.6 per cent of the total HE undergraduate population.

In the area of social class, the profile of Access students is quite distinct from that of the general undergraduate population. UCAS reports, for example, that Access applicants are far more likely than non-Access applicants to be from 'semi-routine occupations' with an 18 per cent proportional difference in this socio-economic category. That same percentage difference is reflected in the much lower proportion of Access students from 'higher managerial and professional' occupations.

The use of the MOSAIC lifestyle analysis, based on neighbourhood types, shows the difference in the socio-economic profile particularly tellingly (QAA 2004c).

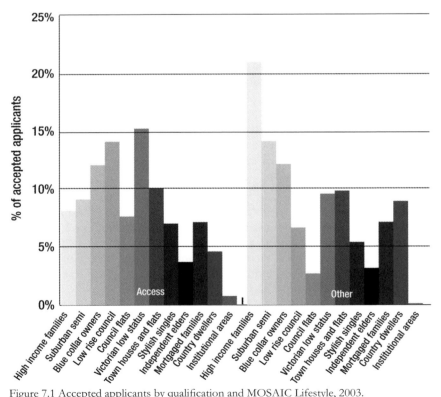

Figure 7.1 Accepted applicants by qualification and MOSAIC Lifestyle, 2003.

It is inevitably the case that more could be done. We might reflect on the differences between application and acceptance statistics for Access students, which appear to show that those in higher social classes are more likely to be accepted than applicants from lower social groups. We might also examine the reasons for the uneven distribution of former Access students in different types of HE institution, with the strong concentration of Access entrants in post-1992 universities. We should attempt to ensure that good practice in one area is extended to other areas, and continue to develop the qualification to ensure that it remains fit for its essential purpose as a preparation for study in HE. Some of these areas will be addressed through QAA's current project for Access, established to take forward the recommendations of last year's development project, as requested in the response from the DfES.

Connectivity

Much developmental activity is best done at the local or regional level. In some parts of the country, connections between Access to HE and other widening participation initiatives, especially those that came about as a result of Partnerships for Progression (P4P) already exist and have provided benefits for both FE and HE partners. Howard Newby's call for connectivity at local and regional level was a reminder that worthwhile widening participation babies should not be thrown out with the P4P bathwater, so we might hope that successful initiatives will be taken forward into the work of lifelong learning networks.

But if some kind of national structure of FE/HE consortia is being sought, with at least one network in each region, as a means of what Newby described as 'delivering post-16 students from under-represented backgrounds to higher education' there is an evident need for connectivity not just at local and regional level but also at national level, with some attention given to the appropriate kinds of connection between a new framework of regional networks for widening participation and any frameworks with related objectives which already exist. In this respect, there is an obvious need for articulation between the work of the AVAs and lifelong learning networks for coherence in this area.

The 'networks'

The national Access framework currently comprises 24 AVAs operating at local and regional level across the whole of England and Wales.[1] There are a number of features of the AVAs which might prove of particular interest in considering how they can contribute to the work of lifelong learning networks.

AVAs are, essentially, consortia of further and higher education institutions, comprising at least two higher education institutions (HEIs), though most have more, and a number of Access providers, most of which are further education colleges (FECs) but which may also include other providers from the voluntary or community sectors, and may also include private training providers. Most HEIs are members of at least one AVA.

Both the FE course providers and HE receivers are required to be involved in developing and validating all QAA-recognised Access courses. It is also a condition of an AVA licence from QAA that both sectors are represented constitutionally within the AVA, to ensure cross-sector involvement in strategic planning and development.

In spite of this emphasis on partnership collaboration, AVAs are required to be independent of any individual institution and to have a small number of professional staff who are accountable to the AVA itself.

New courses are developed by AVAs in response to local demand identified by FECs and to take advantage of opportunities that individual HEIs may be able to offer. The role of the AVA as intermediary or broker between FE providers and HE receivers is particularly critical at a time when FECs have increasing difficulty in finding the resource to support work relating to progression to HE.

AVAs are self-funding through a combination of fees for the validation of courses and associated awards made to students, and membership charges made to partners. Except as being very minor beneficiaries of occasional project funding, AVAs have never received any dedicated resource for development from national initiatives.

Most AVAs are also involved in the accreditation of other courses at a pre-Access level, so that they are able to provide routes through to HE for those who may not yet be ready for Access-level work. The location of most Access courses in FE colleges provides an ease of progression for students starting at a lower level. It is now common for students to progress from 'Access to FE' or 'Return to Learn' courses into Access to HE courses.

AVAs and the Access qualifications they award are all subject to common quality assurance requirements, which give them national recognition through the Access Recognition Scheme. The national recognition of the Access to HE certificate provides students with a qualification which is portable and recognised as an entry qualification throughout the HE sector. This is especially important for the 25 per cent of Access students who go on to institutions which are over 25 miles away from the place where they studied for the Access certificate.

One further distinctive characteristic of AVAs and the Access to HE courses that they recognise is the specific focus on adults. Lifelong learning networks, on the other hand, have broader reference points, and current proposals for lifelong learning networks make little specific reference to adults. Yet the concept of lifelong learning necessarily has implications about the engagement and re-engagement of adults in education: without some reference to what might happen in adulthood, the learning could hardly claim to be lifelong.

The 'lifelong learning'

As a consequence of policy emphases on the 50 per cent participation target for the 18–30 age group, the question of how to engage adults (even those between 19 and 30) as a group which might have specific needs has not played a significant part in the more general debate. A civil servant once suggested to me, apparently seriously, that funding should be withdrawn from Access courses and invested instead in schools-based initiatives, so that no-one would have to go on Access courses in the future. While these ideas have a certain kind of planning logic, as well as an admirable optimism, they also suggest a worrying lack of recognition of the complexity of human motivation and the unpredictability of people's lives and circumstances. There are two problems about this approach: the first is about a commitment to responding to past systemic failings, which have resulted in large numbers of adults with the potential to benefit from HE not having had the opportunity to do so; the second relates to the acknowledgement that it is not only failings in the education system which lead to a failure to progress to university.

Current interventionist strategies, directed primarily at schools, rightly prioritise current problems and attempt to ensure that past failings do not persist. Most adults, however, were at school before the introduction of current initiatives, and many of them have the potential to benefit from higher education. There is both a potential social injustice as well as a wastage of human 'economic resource', if those who had the misfortune to reach school leaving age prior to the introduction of the 50 per cent participation target, and the development of strategies designed to achieve it, should be unable to access the opportunity to go to university which is now offered to those a few years younger.

There is a common view that Access students are mostly people who were denied the opportunity to go to university when younger and have harboured an ambition to do so ever since. Hence the demographic arguments about an imagined falling demand for Access courses because of a supposed diminishing pool of potential Access students. The reality is less straightforward. Many, certainly, were disadvantaged by poor schooling, and most left school with the view that they were not suitably equipped for university. Many will have been affected by personal or family problems, others by larger social problems or cultural attitudes of indifference, if not outright hostility, to education in general, and higher education in particular. Many simply chose to leave school with no intention or desire to progress further. Whatever category or categories they come into they are unlikely to have left with their skills sufficiently well developed to allow them to go straight to university should their circumstances or views of the benefits of education change. There is a danger that the civil servant's approach encourages a 'now or never' structure for progression to higher education, in which it becomes increasingly difficult for adults to find a way back at a later date.

Aside from the fundamental argument about social justice and inclusivity, there are several reasons to consider why adults should be reintroduced into the widening participation debate. The benefits of a strategy which includes specific reference to the needs of adults would be threefold:

(i)   the target for 18–30-year-olds might be more easily met if there were a clear strategy for reaching those between the ages of 19 and 30;

(ii) adults who seek an opportunity to return to education will be able to develop their contribution to society and the economy, and this is likely to be particularly important in the context of changing demography (as clearly argued by NIACE and others); and

(iii) adults have a critical role in the educational 'supply chain': many Access students are or will be parents, or may otherwise have contact with children in areas with low participation in HE.

The importance of parental influence and attitudes, and parents' own educational achievement, is well established in the research about low participation rates. By improving the participation of adults from under-represented groups, the participation of their children becomes more likely, producing both immediate benefits for the parents and longer-term benefits for their children, which would enhance strategies aimed at improving progression at the age of 18.

Some argue that since all entrants to HE are now adults, a distinction between those under and those over the age of 19 is unnecessary and may be unhelpful. However, there is a significant distinction for those attempting to reach under-represented groups between those coming to the end of compulsory education who, on the whole, still live in and are cared for within the parental home, and those who have left school or college some time previously, who probably live independently, and who may have responsibilities for caring for others. In other words, adults are in a different place – literally and metaphorically – from those in school. In order to reach adults, consideration needs to be given to these differences, and distinct approaches may be needed. This is not just about providing a curriculum, teaching and assessment methods which are appropriate for adults, but also about the direction of, and strategies for, targeting and outreach. Pragmatism alone suggests a need for a strategy which includes a specific focus on adults' needs and situations.

While it would make no sense to build an entire policy for widening participation on a 'mop-up' approach, it does make sense to have strategies in place to provide a structural safety net for those significant numbers who do not progress at 18, which would complement the major initiatives designed to improve progression at that age.

A note about vocationalism

Where proposals relating to adults have been made, they have mostly been in the context of the provision of work-based learning and with reference to the development of vocational routes. The proposals from HEFCE and the LSC for lifelong learning networks emphasise their role in relation to vocational progression (HEFCE 2004). This emphasis is reflected in the response from the DfES to QAA's report (DfES 2004). It suggests that lifelong learning networks be encouraged to 'consider the role Access courses currently play in vocational progression to HE and whether and how this might be developed further'.

Many Access students are on Access programmes with an explicitly vocational focus, and the great increase in Access programmes leading to qualifications in health-related professions in recent years, reflected in the 20 per cent of all Access certificates awarded, and of UCAS applications from Access students to subjects allied to medicine, demonstrates the potential of Access to be responsive when demand from students and opportunities in HE, together with the well-advertised needs of a particular employment sector, come together in relation to particular vocational areas.

The proposals also reiterate the functions for lifelong learning networks which were set out by Howard Newby, including the suggestion that they would ensure 'that learners have access to a range of progression opportunities such that they can move between different kinds of vocational and academic programmes as their interests, needs and abilities develop'. Most Access students come to their studies with an essentially vocational long-term purpose – parents wishing to return to employment after a career break; victims of accidents who can no longer continue in their former trade; the unemployed whose skills have become redundant because of technological developments. Some have very clear career plans. Some wish to make further progress in the area in which they are already employed, but others are not in work or may be in a job they wish to leave, perhaps because it offers limited progression opportunities. QAA's recent research on Access illustrated the way in which adults are often trapped by the circumstances of their work, making it impossible for them to take on the study needed for the progression they seek: employers are not always sympathetic to the ambitions of their employees to educate themselves in the substantial kind of way that would be required to move into a graduate position, possibly in a different area of business.

For other students, their understanding of the opportunities available to them and their recognition of their own aptitudes and potential are functions of the educational process itself. The emphasis on vocational education can be problematic if defined too tightly, producing a peculiarly narrow view of what might constitute a 'vocation'. The emphasis on the 'vocational' in HE is reflected in FE in the skills agenda, with its emphasis on skills training and workforce development. For those who are looking for career change or professional development, 'vocational' may mean something rather different.

Finally

Access to HE has stood on the sidelines of widening participation policy, as initiatives to improve the progression of young people have developed and become more embedded in educational practice. QAA has willingly held the responsibility for managing and regulating the framework for Access courses recognition throughout this period. In that time, new AVA licensing and review methods have been developed, implemented and evaluated, and a further process of development – which is likely to make some radical changes to the qualification itself – is now under way.

The AVAs have developed a great deal since the early 1990s: they have become larger, better able to support developmental activity, and more professional in their role as awarding bodies. The Access courses themselves have developed in their structure and content. They have provided a wider range of opportunities, in more flexible ways, in order to respond to the needs of different target groups and changing opportunities for progression into HE. Most significantly, somewhere in the region of 80,000 adults have been enabled to enter higher education, most of whom would probably not otherwise have done so.

It is remarkable that a case has to be made to demonstrate the nature of the contribution of Access to HE or to argue for its inclusion in national strategies which have the same aim as Access has held for the last 25 years. But, like the kid in the park who is left holding the ball when his mates go off to explore some other exciting development elsewhere, those involved in Access have watched with bemusement and wondered whether anyone would ever come back for the ball. Now that there is some new activity at the other end of the park, which seems to share many of the same players and characteristics as the original game, it seems only sensible to enquire whether we might join forces. At this point, perhaps we should at least look at how much we have in common, and, if we have much the same purpose, see how the players might usefully be brought together in pursuing common goals.

Note

1   The number has fallen in recent years, as mergers have resulted in larger, stronger groupings.

References

Department for Education and Employment (DfEE) (1987) *Higher Education Meeting the Challenge*. London: HMSO.

Department for Education and Skills (DfES) (2003) *The Future of Higher Education*. London: The Stationery Office.

Newby, Sir Howard (2005) 'Doing Widening Participation: Social Inequality and Access to Higher Education' (Colin Bell Memorial Lecture, University of Bradford March 2004), in G. Layer (ed.), *Closing the Equity Gap: Impact of Widening Participation Strategies in the UK and the USA*. Leicester: NIACE.

Quality Assurance Agency for Higher Education (QAA) (2004a) *Access to Higher Education Development Project*. Gloucester: QAA.

Quality Assurance Agency (QAA) (2004b) (Department for Education and Skills response to QAA Review of Access Courses). www.qaa.ac.uk/crntwork/access/developmentproject/dfesresponse

Quality Assurance Agency (QAA) (2004c) www.qaa.ac.uk/crntwork/access/statistics/2004/stats_2004_UCAS_report

CHAPTER EIGHT

Going with the grain? Some notes and queries on lifelong learning networks

Robert G. Burgess

While the concept of *lifelong learning* has been around for a long time, the policy of a lifelong learning network has emerged as part of the Higher Education Funding Council for England (HEFCE)'s policy over the last twelve months. In particular, Howard Newby filled in the detail of what might constitute a lifelong learning network in his Colin Bell Memorial Lecture in Bradford in March 2004. Essentially, lifelong learning networks would link together further education colleges and higher education institutions across a city, a region or area and would offer a wide-ranging curriculum. This, it was argued, would bring together higher and further education. The key concept that was used in relation to the network was 'progression'; that is the idea that there would be clear pathways for learners moving from further education into higher education in a particular region. In part, the idea appears to have its genesis in models of higher education in the United States where relationships are firmly established within particular areas between universities and community colleges.

However, the way in which the policy has been interpreted means that rather than many different models being possible, it appears to have been translated into a set of rather fixed views with certain 'models' being seen as most appropriate for particular regions. In this respect, it is appropriate to raise a series of questions about lifelong learning networks. Among the key questions that should be placed high on the agenda are:

- What constitutes lifelong learning when discussed in relation to a network?
- Is it that lifelong learning networks can only be linked to the nine English regions or sub-regions, or is it more appropriate that lifelong learning networks cross different geographical areas, bringing together groups that have some academic and professional affinity?
- Is it appropriate that lifelong learning networks should only focus on progression? There are many other activities that could be associated with groups of further and higher education colleges coming together, for example staff development, further training, joint courses and so on.

Already it is apparent that a number of questions and queries can be raised about the concept of a lifelong learning network but, most importantly, it would seem that in the policies that have been enunciated there is an assumption that very little work has been done in this area. Yet we can point to much evidence of further education and higher education working together through a series of networks that have coalesced around particular higher education institutions. In this respect, a number of questions need to be raised about what might constitute a lifelong learning network.

Further information about the networks has been provided in correspondence from HEFCE and the Learning and Skills Council. Indeed, it is acknowledged that HEFCE, the Learning and Skills Council and the Department for Education and Skills (DfES) have been working together to encourage progression into and through higher education so that lifelong learning networks might be seen as part of the widening participation agenda and, in turn, vehicles for broadening access into higher education. In addition, it is argued that lifelong learning networks are a means of collaboration with partners at regional and local level but with a focus on vocational progression. This raises further questions. First, what constitutes progression? Secondly, why is progression in a lifelong learning network to be limited to vocational work? What counts as vocationalism? How is it being interpreted in relation to lifelong learning?

Further information identifies a number of attributes of lifelong learning networks. The characteristics of the networks would include:

- Combining the strengths of a number of diverse institutions. But, we might ask, has this not been successfully done to date? Why might such institutions need to be regionally or sub-regionally based?
- Providing support for learners on vocational pathways. Here we might acknowledge that it is important that different institutions provide support for learners, but why is it restricted to vocational areas? This suggests that lifelong learning is equated with vocationalism, which I am sure we would need to question.
- Providing greater clarity, coherence and certainty to progression opportunities. This assumes that there is little by way of development in respect of compacts between colleges and universities, yet one can point to a diverse network of opportunities that exist in different areas of the country. Obviously there is not necessarily nationwide coherence in provision, but there is much work that has already taken place.
- Developing a curriculum appropriate to facilitate progression. Once again, there is an assumption here that appears to rest on the view that there is very little work that has been done to develop curricula and pedagogy in relation to learner progression. Yet there is evidence of groups of staff from higher and further education coming together with a view to discussing issues of curriculum content and pedagogic style.
- Valuing vocational learning and providing opportunities for vocational learners to build on earlier learning. This appears to assume that vocational learners have few opportunities provided for them, and that there are few links between the learning that occurs in schools and colleges and that in higher education.

- Locating the progression strategy within a commitment to lifelong learning which would ensure that learners have access to a range of progression opportunities, moving between vocational and academic programmes. Once again, a series of assumptions appear to be made, especially about the use of opportunities within and beyond lifelong learning networks.

A brief analysis of the issues associated with lifelong learning networks seems to suggest that there are a number of assumptions and problems associated with the operationalisation and implementation of some aspects of lifelong learning policy in relation to lifelong learning networks. Furthermore, there is a danger that if these networks are to be based only in geographical regions they will omit some areas of work that have been successfully developed over the last few years.

A Colleges-University network

In this section of the chapter, I briefly sketch some of the work that has been developed in a Colleges-University of Leicester network that has been in existence over the last five years.

On joining the University of Leicester six years ago, it seemed to me very appropriate that a University that claimed to be excellent in research and teaching should bring another dimension to its work by making links with colleges in the locality. Accordingly, arrangements were made to establish links with sixth-form colleges and colleges of further education that were in the vicinity of the University. This began with a group that gradually built to a critical size of 14 institutions. Some of the activities that were developed within this group included the following:

- The development of training through shared staff development.
- The development of links through Foundation Degrees.
- The development of work associated with one-year pre-University foundation programmes.
- The development of shared resources, such as libraries.
- The development of policy, for example sustainability in further and higher education.

In this respect, the work of the network went well beyond some of the areas that are specified as part of a lifelong learning network. However, it could be argued that the colleges network did not focus on progression as a central theme but rather picked up a number of themes and topics that could be explored.

Subsequently, the University held discussions with two colleges of higher education who were interested in developing a validation relationship with the institution and, in turn, a further set of relationships that we summarised as 'validation plus' were developed. While validation arrangements with Newman College in the West Midlands and Bishop Grosseteste College in the East Midlands continued to develop apace, we also explored other possibilities. These included:

- Staff from the colleges working jointly with University staff in terms of research activity.
- Sharing staff development.
- Sharing and using each other's sites.
- Developing research supervision whereby College staff worked jointly with University staff on the provision of doctoral training and supervision.
- Developing relationships between further education colleges that were associated with the two colleges of higher education by bringing them all into the Colleges-University of Leicester network.

The result of this activity is that we have increased the size of the Colleges-University of Leicester network so that it now consists of 23 institutions (20 sixth-form and further education colleges, together with two colleges of higher education and the University). It is evident that such a network requires human resources in order to develop the range of work, and an essential ingredient is time. At the moment it has been successful through support provided from the Learning and Skills Council and by each institution. But fundamentally it relies on the enthusiasm and commitment of staff from the member institutions. Obviously, there are costs associated with the time it takes to travel between the institutions that lie between Birmingham and Scunthorpe.

The work that has been completed links with some aspects of a lifelong learning network. However, there is other work that members of the Colleges-University of Leicester network wish to develop. This includes:

- The creation of an electronic contact directory in order to provide basic information about staff contacts within each of the member institutions so that it is easy for someone who wishes to discuss the curriculum in, say, English to rapidly identify all those involved across all the institutions.
- Support and encouragement of further education–higher education action research clusters. In this instance, different groups have worked together to begin an audit of activity that would result in further developments across the network. In particular, health and social care has been supported by the Workforce Development Confederation. Meanwhile, work in the field of modern and community languages has been carried out with support from an external language-based group.
- Improvement in learners' transition and progression arrangements. Already much work has taken place involving the University's widening participation team. This has included discussions about cluster arrangements in order that the Leicestershire Progression Accord could be re-focused within the network.

- Better sharing of information on Foundation Degree developments. Here, there has been coordination between the different institutions on the proposed provision of Foundation Degrees so that collaboration can be explored. However, a number of obstacles have also been identified, including the use of staff time, the lack of resources, and funding problems. In this respect, the issues relate very much to the problems more generally associated with collaboration between a range of institutions.
- The development of different networking models. Already the network has explored different models of working together in order to address issues of geography and travel time among its members.

This brief summary of some of the work that has been conducted in the Colleges-University of Leicester network suggests that there is already a series of issues that can be clearly identified and articulated about the problems associated with colleges and universities working together. Obviously, much benefit has been derived from working in collaboration, but it is important not to overlook some of the obvious problems that have been identified. So we might ask, what might be the implications for the development of a lifelong learning network? What can be learned from our experience in developing a Colleges-University network?

Towards a lifelong learning network

At this point, comments on babies and bathwater might seem appropriate advice for HEFCE. There is much work that needs to be developed out of collaborative partnerships in further and higher education. There are also several areas that require exploration:

- It is vital that we understand the work that is being currently conducted in colleges and universities; existing networks need to be mapped.
- The way in which that work can be supported and sustained needs to be explored.
- Ways in which lifelong learning networks might not be narrowly defined in terms of vocational orientations to progression need to be examined.
- Finally, we need to build upon good practice.

It is to be hoped that our discussions will result in reinvigorating the concept of a lifelong learning network in order that it can fully sustain the rich range of activities that could be associated with such networks, and realise the potential of further and higher education working in collaboration. In short, it is essential to go with the grain and build upon much work that is already in existence, and that needs to be developed and sustained.

CHAPTER NINE

Lifelong interrupted

David Vincent

The turning-point was Howard Newby's Colin Bell Memorial Lecture in March of this year (Newby 2005). Howard Newby and Colin Bell, who died in harness at Stirling in 2003, had started their careers together in the sociology department at Essex, then, as now, one of the most influential centres of the discipline in the country. They represented the advanced guard of the infiltration of the ranks of vice-chancellors by the new university departments of the 1960s and 1970s. No longer was it necessary to have run an engineering or medical school to aspire to senior management. The history men were taking over direction of the history of higher education. It was now possible to move, in Newby's case, from the deferential rural worker to chief executive, and in Bell's case from the middle-class family to the head of universities on both sides of the border.

Such careers were framed by an engagement with social class. In his memorial lecture, Newby was able to make a plausible case for Colin Bell and by extension for himself as lifelong warriors against inherited privilege. Through their teaching, their research, and eventually their management roles they had embodied a commitment to the role of education in promoting equality of life chances. But Newby's lecture was much more than an extended obituary, a discourse on how to be both an intellectual iconoclast and an organisation man in the era of mass participation. It was a deliberate intervention in a particular moment in the politics of higher education in the first decade of the new century.

The lecture sought to do two things. The first was to reassure those who feared that the looming prospect of top-up fees represented a betrayal of the ideals of equality of opportunity to which he and Bell and so much of the academic profession had been committed. 'One of the most frequently quoted and perhaps most compelling reasons for widening participation', he argued, 'is the increased private rate of return to graduates.' While he remained sufficient of a professional researcher to doubt the precision of the figures being cited, he did accept the general force of the argument. It was a reason why students should pay such fees, and a further incentive for encouraging those from poorer backgrounds to enjoy the lifelong benefits of gaining a degree.

The second was to push the debate beyond the figure of the full-time school-leaver and his or her willingness to pay for a university education. 'As we move from an elite to a more mass higher education system,' he wrote, 'it is unreasonable to believe that we will succeed simply by offering 'more of the same'.' The ambitions of vice-chancellors to get money into their institutions from any available source in order to pay their bills did not themselves constitute a sufficient agenda for higher education in the new century. Larger goals remained: 'as higher education moves from being a 'once-in-a-lifetime' opportunity to a lifelong requirement which needs to be refreshed and updated across a lifetime, so it needs to be delivered in a more flexible, student-centred form – part-time as well as full-time, in the workplace, on-line, via distance learning, and so forth.' He was seeking to put time back into widening participation, and flexibility back into higher education.

In one sense, Newby's endorsement of flexible, student-centred, lifelong learning was a little too early. The agitation for top-up fees was still travelling towards its theatrical finale and the educational press had little time for more contemplative discussions of the means and ends of the university system. Eventually, however, the storm blew itself out. The Government moved on to different parts of the public sector, and their Members of Parliament turned their attention to the really great issues of the era, such as fox-hunting and roulette tables. At the 2004 Labour Party Conference in Brighton there were more stalls on free Tibet (two) than on higher education (none). Only NIACE was conspicuous by its presence. At this moment of calm, Newby's attempt to reverse higher education policy out of the cul-de-sac into which it had been driven began to seem more relevant. His central message was deeply familiar to everyone at the NIACE 2004 Seminar. It was only made radical by the two-year lapse of attention among vice-chancellors and the Department for Education and Skills which began with the blinkered White Paper of 2003 and ended with the knife-edge votes in the Commons.

Just how far the bulk of vice-chancellors are prepared to distract themselves from the vision of all those £3,000 cheques and pay attention to this reawakened ambition remains to be seen. It has to be recognised that a strong motive for engaging in widening participation activity in the past five years was that it offered cash-strapped institutions one of the very few avenues to new money and new students. None of us can estimate the precise impact of this gamble with the Government's social justice agenda.

In the new higher education economy there are likely to be more than a few universities currently reviewing the financial and opportunity costs of engaging in forms of outreach work that in real terms frequently failed to pay its way. When the Russell Group speaks of broadening the current framework it means removing the £3,000 ceiling on fees. The Government has set up the Office for Fair Access (OFFA) to try to prevent the sector abandoning widening participation altogether, but the indications are that most of the teeth of this new body have already been drawn. It is a worrying sign that the recent onslaught by the incoming Chancellor of Oxford University on the whole concept of 'social engineering' through admissions policies was met by a hasty denial by the incoming Minister of Higher Education that he or his Government had any such intention.

There will nonetheless be universities which will want to take this seriously, partly because of their genuine commitment to the mission and partly because Newby is not just another sociologist and undoubtedly intends that the Higher

Education Funding Council for England (HEFCE) contributes to and if necessary enforces change in this arena. The issue for this volume is how far we should welcome the vision set out in Newby's lecture and subsequently embodied in a joint circular from HEFCE and the Learning and Skills Council (LSC) on 3 June 2004. The circular, entitled 'lifelong learning networks', envisages 'groups of institutions, including higher education institutions (HEIs) and further education colleges (FECs), that come together across a city, area or region to offer new progression opportunities for vocational learners'. One of the purposes of this initiative is to 'locate the progression strategy within a commitment to lifelong learning, ensuring that learners have access to a range of progression opportunities so that they can move between different kinds of vocational and academic programmes as their interests, needs and abilities develop' (HEFCE 2004, para. 2).

Within the framework of the renewed commitment to lifelong learning, there are three obvious grounds for optimism. First, the policy represents yet another version of the long line of initiatives stretching back at least as far as the invention of secondary modern schools to establish parity of esteem for vocational education. There is a specific intention to close the large gap between progression rates to higher education from vocational programmes and those from conventional academic qualifications. The publication of the Tomlinson Report represented a kind of second front in the same battle.

Secondly, it constitutes a genuine effort to articulate all the players in the confused and confusing space through which learners must find their way as they raise their aspirations and their achievements. The fact that the policy document was signed by both HEFCE and the LSC was both a symbolic and a practical statement of the need to work across the traditional boundaries in post-13 education.

Thirdly, the policy acknowledges that a student-centred approach needs to be responsive to learner needs in terms of mode of delivery. It recognises that provision needs to be 'part-time or full-time, delivered on campus (including outreach locations) or through distance learning, including e-learning, or some combination of these' (HEFCE 2004, Annex A, para. 27).

It is, however, possible to argue that the policy represents at best a half-hearted attempt to change the parameters of lifelong learning. It looks more like an attempt to repair the rust in a car that has been off the road for a few years than a radical redesign of new vehicle. There are several grounds for caution.

The first is that of language. Circular 12/2004 refers in its first sentence to 'joint approaches to encouraging progression into and through higher education' (HEFCE 2004, para. 1). As the earlier quotation indicated, the language of progression infuses the document. A truly student-centred engagement with lifelong learning will always have difficulty with the relentlessly hierarchical terminology in which the enterprise continues to be expressed. For a given student, a return to learning must always be an expression of some kind of ambition and the completion of a programme some kind of achievement. There is, however, no necessary reason why intention and outcome should be described in terms of a numerical advance. In some cases there certainly will be students who are seeking to overcome obstacles to move from one level of study to another, although a central characteristic of this progression may be its deeply punctuated movement. For many others, however, there is little or no sense of this kind of ascending.

There is a species of Open University (OU) student which is, in these terms, deliberately and cheerfully travelling in circles, getting to the end of a diploma or a degree and starting off again in another subject. There are others picking up courses or modules here and there and quite properly resisting all encouragement to 'build' them into something larger. For continuing professional development (CPD) students' progress tends to be in terms of keeping an existing level of attainment in a discipline up to date and in formal terms working repeatedly at the same level. For others again progress is simply broadening skills or satisfying intellectual curiosity whether this means taking a General Certificate of Secondary Education (GSCE) in a language at having gained a degree half a lifetime ago, or adding a qualification in cabinet-making to a Ph.D. in astrophysics.

This *normative language* is embedded in the conventional educational sector, with its cardinal qualifications frameworks and its ordinal structure of primary, secondary and tertiary. *Tertiary* is itself a more inclusive term than *higher*. Those of us based south of the border have watched with wry amusement the recent doomed attempt by the Scottish Executive to replace the latter term by the former as its seeks to bring the further education and university sectors under one administrative roof. The language is inherently patronising and confining. It is a vision of a ladder, the top end of which is being held by the traditional university sector, which, in the perspective of this Labour Government certainly has its own top and bottom ends.

Ironically, it is a vision confined to a cohort of the population which has scarcely begun to live its adult lives. In respect of the existing providers of the part-time, flexible, vocational education whom Newby seeks to embrace, it means signing up to an agenda defined by the struggle to get young men and women out of unconventional lower educational structures and into higher conventional ones. Such a conception ill accords with the language of the Circular. 'Above all', it proclaims, ' the LLN will add value because it is learner centred, and learner driven' (HEFCE 2004, Annex A, para. 12). A truly learner-centred project must be founded on the learner's own definition of progress and success.

The second problem is one of coverage. In his lecture, Newby quite properly deplores the sheer incoherence of the contemporary landscape: 'the vocational pathway is neither clear nor consistently applied. It varies enormously from one part of the country to another and it is therefore simply not clear to a sixteen year old what this pathway is and where it will lead. This is a travesty of modern higher education which would scarcely be tolerated in any of our major industrial competitors.' However, the subsequent Circular which seeks to turn the analysis into action goes out of its way to avoid any semblance of creating a new system. 'We do not expect every network to be the same', it assures universities, 'and want to encourage innovative approaches to developing and supporting progression for vocational learners. In some areas, LLNs will build on existing arrangements and relationships, while in others there may be new possibilities that can be explored. Networks will also develop at different speeds . . .' (HEFCE 2004, para. 6). There is not even to be a formal bidding process for funds. The form of request is flexible, and just in case universities feel they are being hustled into doing anything in particular, the Circular adds that it is anxious 'not to constrain development by artificial deadlines' (HEFCE 2004, para. 8).

My analogy of a car seriously overstates the sophistication of this vehicle. It is more a collection of children meeting in different places to hammer together carts out of whatever recycled materials they can find lying around. Thus the OU learns through its regional offices that in the south-east Kent is taking the lead and Sussex may be getting something together; in the south-west Bristol and Bath are thought to be working up their own bids and Bournemouth is leading a large collaborative venture; in the East Midlands there is a Coalfields Alliance Sub-Regional Strategic Partnership in the Nottinghamshire and Derbyshire Coalfield, and another network planned for Nottinghamshire as a whole; the east is planning a kind of matrix of networks, some thematically based, others spatially; in Yorkshire, which already has its own networks, there is general suspicion of the disorder the new policy may bring; in the north-east, the existing structure of Universities for the North East decided not to get involved but let individual institutions do their own thing.

It is evident that no-one in HEFCE is seeking to win the Robespierre of the Month award. This approach can be praised for its desire not to override the achievements which have already been put in place, and for its sensitivity to the complex local politics which will determine the limits of the possible in particular areas. But set against Newby's test for a satisfactory environment for the vocational student, or any others seeking to make their way out of a disadvantaged background, this is confusion further confounded. The only certain outcome of this Circular is that the provision will be more heterogeneous in the medium term than it is now. A parallel might be drawn with the National Health Service, which has its problems with consistency of access across the country and between social classes. At least there is an attempt at national provision, and acceptance that its absence is a basic measure of failure.

The reason for the disorder in higher education is not a lack of will on the part of HEFCE, but rather a recognition of the limits to its power. This partly relates to relations between HEFCE and the chartered universities. Having won their money and fought to keep OFFA at bay, vice-chancellors are in no mood to be dragooned into a single model of a lifelong learning framework. And it partly relates to the weakness of HEFCE within the world which it is now trying to pattern. It is one thing to drive for a single reform which involves only the players within the university sector. It is quite another building an alliance out of disparately funded and managed bodies not all of which are subject to control by the Department for Education and Skills. The tendency for joint enterprises to be based on the lowest common denominator seems to be in play here. The irony is that the lifelong learning networks are intended not only to bring coherence to a rapid burgeoning of regional bodies and strategies but also to try to integrate the many initiatives that HEFCE itself visited upon the HE sector – CVEs, CETLs, NTIs, Knowledge Exchanges, Aimhigher partnerships, and so on.

The third problem is the structure identified as the answer to the second. The lifelong learning networks may take this or that form over this or that period of time, but it is intended that they will develop 'in individual regions' in conjunction with 'regional and local partners' (HEFCE 2004, paras. 2, 4). HEFCE's regional consultants and the LSC's regional directors are supposed to instil some order into the emerging initiatives, and all the structures will be integrated with the developing framework of regional government in which the LSCs are already embedded. This is again a piece of *realpolitik*. The regions are held to understand local need better than Whitehall or Bristol. They are in possession of a wealth of strategic statements and analyses of need, to say nothing of increasing income flows. They provide an arena in which different elements of the public and sometimes the private sector can work together. All conventional universities belong to regional HE bodies which are to be closely involved in this strategy, and most national providers of flexible learning, including the OU, already have regional structures which map onto the system of devolved government.

Yet if we gaze at this world through the eyes of the lifelong student, this is neither a sufficient nor an effective framework for realising their aspirations. Regional government in England makes the European Union (EU) look like an Athenian democracy. There is minimal local accountability, a yawning gulf between grandiloquent mission and measured outcomes, and despite the pretence of cartographical coverage, major inconsistencies in their focus of attention. In general, the largest cities in the centre of the regions have been far more successful in constructing proto-networks than more scattered towns and in particular than the rural areas. A body such as the Greater Manchester Strategic Alliance has the potential to confer real benefit on a large population, but it does not stand in for a coherent provision across Lancashire, let alone the North-West more broadly.

A lifelong learning strategy which ignores regional government is inconceivable; a strategy which is confined to the regions is ineffective. This is because there remain other spatial and structural dimensions to the issue. It is a matter of the boundaries of legitimate variation. Students need the players in their local area to be working together, and may well want to make direct use of their facilities. On the other hand they have no use for qualification frameworks which work only in a 50-mile radius of their home, nor for curricula which fit them only for employment in the surrounding economy, nor, and this is a major weakness of the current system, for so-called progression routes which channel them straight into the arms of the hungriest university in their area. The concept of a learning community has great pedagogic power within the world of continuing education. There is no particular reason why it should be coextensive with a region or any sub-framework within it.

In accordance with the non-systematic nature of the enterprise, the strategy does allow for various special formats within the regions. But if there is some recognition of the local within the regional, there is none of entities larger than the region. At the very least there needs to be a greater sense of *variable geometry* in the provision of lifelong learning, capable of adjustment to the local when it needs to be specific to the student's home, to the region when it needs a greater level of resource and coordination, and to the national or international when it needs economies of scale and the kind of boundless mobility of mind and body which the dream of lifelong learning has always proffered. It may be noted that the Bologna Process, another event ignored by the 2003 White Paper and the top-up fee debate, now specifically endorses lifelong learning as an objective of the EU.

Contributors to this symposium will represent different positions in terms of these levels. A number will be like the OU, able to deliver very localised services, prepared to participate in regional initiatives, but most of all seeking to provide a national infrastructural service to the new enterprise. There is a place for overarching resources in managing qualifications frameworks, operating credit transfer systems, supplying the components of distance-learning curricula, and providing online student services. What are needed are not just partnerships between neighbouring players, but vertical relationships in which regional and local bodies can draw down such facilities as they need, to achieve efficiency of operation and provide some semblance of a consistent service to all those seeking to move between different forms and levels of education throughout their learning lives.

References

Higher Education Funding Council for England (HEFCE) (2004) *Joint Letter from HEFCE and the Learning and Skills Council*, HEFCE Circular 12/2004. Bristol: HEFCE.

Newby, Howard (2005) 'Doing Widening Participation: Social Inequality and Access to Higher Education', Colin Bell Memorial Lecture, March 2004, in G. Layer (ed.), *Closing the Equity Gap: Impact of Widening Participation Strategies in the UK and the USA*. Leicester: NIACE.

Possible futures

CHAPTER TEN

Lifelong learning networks, vocational learners, and progression

Kevin Whitston

Lifelong learning networks (LLNs) aim to bring the same opportunity, coherence and certainty to the higher education experience of vocational learners as is enjoyed by their academic counterparts. A brief tour of the historical context of vocational learning will show why this is necessary, and will indicate what LLNs need to do to achieve these aims.

Vocational training and education has been a sorry second best in Britain. Old-style apprenticeship was once the royal route into skilled employment, surviving longer in Britain than most places. But as early as the 1920s, in the new mass-production sectors, apprenticeship had all but disappeared, and decline from the 1960s has been rapid (Gospel 1994; McKinlay 1991). The number of apprentices almost halved during the ten-year life of the Industrial Training Boards set up in 1963 (Owen 1991, p. 411). According to one account, by the time its successor the Manpower Services Commission was wound up in 1988 'skills training in British industry all but ceased' (Ainley 1993, p. 45). Training and Education Councils, now part of the Learning and Skills Council (LSC), were next into the lists, and National Vocational Qualifications (NVQs), the new employer-led competence-based qualifications, became the new vocational offer. Students, argues Alison Wolf, voted with their feet, opting instead for traditional academic qualifications. By 1996 there were 800 NVQs; but 42 of these accounted for 83 per cent of certificates awarded. And 364 never awarded a single certificate to a single candidate (Wolf 2002, p. 76).

If students were voting for traditional academic qualifications it was because they had little choice. Britain never developed a broadly based education offer in the school or higher education sector. The 1944 Education Act established grammar, technical, and secondary modern schools to go with its underpinning vision of 'gold, silver and iron' children but technical schools never established themselves. Comprehensive reorganisation was carried out on the basis of the grammar school curriculum, and all subsequent attempts to provide a vocational learning option have run into the sand. Most recently Advanced General National Vocational Qualifications (AGNVQs) have been replaced by the Advanced Vocational Certificate of Education (AVCE); this has continued to edge closer to traditional A levels and will shortly become the Advanced Certificate of Education in different subject areas. In 2004 The

Office for Standards in Education, Ofsted, issued a critical if contested report that found AVCEs insufficiently vocational for vocational purposes, and insufficiently academic for academic ones.

Employers haven't always helped. Sanderson argues that the failure to develop technical education for non-academic teenagers played a significant part in British economic decline, but he notes too the absence of demand from employers for those with a technical education, or for graduates (Sanderson 1988; 1972). Leverhulme preferred the 'hard-knocks graduate'; Morris didn't like graduates at all. At Vickers in the 1930s people with a degree kept quiet about it for fear of getting the sack (Pagnamenta and Overy 1984, p. 272). Where graduates were welcome it was as much for their character and social skills as the knowledge they had acquired in higher education (Keeble 1992). Nor was this a judgement applied only to graduates. So-called skill shortages often boiled down to 'desirable behaviours' rather than 'cognitive ability or manual dexterity'; what Oliver and Turton (1982) called the 'good bloke syndrome'. It is not wholly surprising that one investigator in the 1960s, Professor Zuckerman, declared that 'we discovered in our successive enquiries that one of the least reliable ways of finding out what industry needs is to go and ask industry' (see Keeble 1992, p. 89).

Perhaps matters have not been quite as bad as this thumbnail sketch suggests. A great deal of early vocational education and training took place in a variety of voluntary institutes quite outside the formal system. There were good reasons why British employers rejected the elaborate German model of vocational training (Pollard 1989, p. 178). Technical and further education colleges offered, and continue to offer, a bewildering variety of professional and vocational qualifications. City and Guilds and BTEC programmes at level 3 have been consistently well regarded, as have Higher National Certificates and Diplomas.

But the school curriculum is still narrowly based and the connection between even the most firmly established vocational qualifications and entry to, and progression within, higher education is tenuous or uncertain. The data are poor – and the Higher Education Funding Council for England (HEFCE) is working with the Department for Education and Skills and the LSC to rectify this – but the progression rate into higher education for those with level-3 vocational qualifications is much lower than for those with traditional A levels.

Once in higher education the opportunity of further progression is arbitrary. Where specific articulation arrangements have been agreed between colleges and higher education institutions (HEIs) progression is smooth enough. In other cases moving from higher education (HE) programmes in further education (FE) to HE programmes offered in HEIs is negotiated on a case-by-case basis (Greenwood, Parry et al. 2002, p. 3). Where progression is available, vocational learners are often confronted with unfamiliar teaching and learning styles, or a vocational curriculum that has been distorted to fit the pattern of progression on offer (Little et al. 2000).

Finally, there is a substantial number of vocational learners whose learning doesn't fit any established pattern at all. About 63,000 students are enrolled on

NVQ levels 4/5 or other advanced higher-level vocational qualifications in non-prescribed higher education (Parry *et al.* 2003, p. 6). Developed in a creative and chaotic way by professional bodies, sometimes sanctioned by the Curriculum Qualifications Authority and delivered in FE, even the status of this work as HE is uncertain. In some ways it provides a fitting comment on the marginal place of vocational learning more generally.

At the beginning of the twentieth century the new civic universities brought the vocations associated with the science and technology of the second industrial revolution into the academy. At the beginning of the twenty-first century higher education needs to make a comparable adjustment, extending higher-level learning to a wider community of vocational learners. The need for greater opportunity, coherence and certainty is pretty clear. Can lifelong learning networks contribute to this?

Lifelong learning networks (LLNs) and a lifelong learning HE offer

Recent developments could bring a new coherence for vocational learners. Employer engagement is being sought via new sector skills councils. Advanced modern apprenticeships (now simply called apprenticeships) introduced in the early 1990s could offer work-based learning to around a quarter of young people. Over the next ten years Tomlinson could create, for the first time, a broadly based curriculum offer in schools. The Qualifications and Curriculum Authority (QCA) is working to roughly the same timetable. The new standards, qualifications and systems generated by the Framework for Achievement should be introduced between 2006 and 2010. The new Foundation Degree already offers work-based and work-related higher education opportunities.

There is a danger of course that all this serves to introduce into Britain a parallel vocationally focused education system designed for the last century just at the time when others are moving in the opposite direction. Wolf, for example, argues that in Europe the content of the vocational track is changing to become more general and academic; that youngsters are only attracted to vocational programmes when they are linked to HE (Wolf 2002, p. 88). New technology and changing occupational structures make the old mental/manual division of labour, and the academic/vocational distinction attached to it, all the more shaky. As learners who have started out on a vocational pathway develop their knowledge, skills and abilities they need to develop their capacity to step back and reflect, to analyse and to reason. And as those who started out on an academic pathway will quickly discover, they will need to turn reason and reflection to practical purposes.

At the same time the tension between 'academic-vocational' will not simply go away, nor will an undifferentiated curriculum serve the interests of a wider range of learners. Much depends on how the new initiatives work out. Tomlinson will have to provide more opportunity for vocational learning without confining that learner to narrow and pre-determined pathways. Apprenticeships will need to link academic to practical, applied learning. Foundation Degrees will need to be employment-related, not focused on particular skills or specific jobs. Better access to higher education for vocational learners must mean opportunities to build on earlier learning rather than being pitched into an unsuitable programme for which they are unprepared. At the same time improved access must not confine people to the particular starting-point in their journey.

Lifelong learning networks seek to address these tensions in two ways; first by involving HEIs from across the sector, including the most research-intensive, and secondly by linking new HE opportunities for vocational learners to lifelong learning.

The institutional patterns we create should not reinforce the stereotypes that are all too easy to construct. As people grow and develop the whole of the higher education offer must be available to them. No programme or institution should be off-limits. That is why LLNs should involve research-intensive HEIs as well as those with a much stronger track record in making higher education available to vocational learners. LLNs will bring together different HEIs and colleges, creating a network that reconnects the sector for the purposes of progression at a time when market pressures stemming from the introduction of variable fees threaten to pull it apart. And because progression is firmly located in a lifelong-learning perspective, different sorts of learners can access a wide range of programmes as their lives and careers unfold.

The use of the words 'lifelong learning' in connection with the proposed networks has attracted some criticism. Some suggest that it is inappropriate for an initiative too narrowly concerned with vocational progression and a focus on qualifications. It is unquestionably the case that lifelong learning networks do not cover the whole lifelong learning ground. They are certainly not synonymous with lifelong learning as such. However, there are few initiatives that hit all the lifelong learning buttons. What can confidently be claimed for networks is that they make a contribution to lifelong learning because they put the re-engagement of the learner centre-stage.

Networks are not simply about access, an initial experience of higher education for vocational learners. Nor are they about progression in the simple sense of climbing to the top of an educational *ladder*, however defined. The networks aim to provide a *net*, a framework of educational opportunity, to address the way the educational needs of vocational learners change as their needs, interests and abilities change. To secure this, networks will identify ways of supporting and re-engaging learners over a lifetime, providing 'personalised learning', negotiated learning pathways that help learners plan and manage their long-term as well as short-term learning goals.

Building on what exists

The consultation that HEFCE and the LSC have initiated through their regional teams is a relatively open one. There is no single model for a lifelong learning network, and institutions have not, therefore, been invited to bid for a defined pot of money, with bids scored against strictly defined criteria. A more developmental dialogue is needed that can explore initial proposals and develop these further through consultation and negotiation. The starting-point must be what potential networks wish to propose, and what they believe they can deliver. On that basis different models can emerge to serve as 'pilots' or 'demonstrators'.

Three closely related concerns have been raised about this process. The first is that lifelong learning networks should build on existing networks and relationships and that whatever happens they must not undermine the positive work that is already being done. The second is the worry that lifelong learning networks will add yet another layer of complexity; that they will contribute to 'partnership fatigue'. Finally, there are questions about the spatial boundaries of LLNs, given the region-led consultation.

As argued above, LLNs will distinguish themselves by forging vocational progression routes with colleges and HEIs from across the whole sector. The early indications are that they will do so by building on, and extending, existing partnership initiatives. This is the case in the North-East where a number of HEI-college consortia have been brought together, in Manchester and York where lifelong learning networks are being aligned with pre-existing strategic alliances, and in Sussex where a lifelong learning network is described as a 'partnership of partnerships'.

Not every HEI-college network will be accommodated in this way. Even if it could, there will be partnerships where links and working relationships are such that participants do not want to change them. They may feel that they already provide good progression opportunities and can build on these without adopting the LLN form. There is no reason why LLNs should interfere with or undermine these arrangements, which are in any case underpinned by the Funding Councils in various ways. LLNs will add to this provision, not diminish it.

There is an expectation that most LLNs will be made up of local clusters of institutions but there are no requirements laid down about this. In fact there are proposals coming forward for national networks and for networks that cross regional boundaries. Others encompass a whole region or links between institutions in sub-regional clusters. If a proposed network makes sense in terms of geographical or communications links it doesn't matter if it isn't confined to regional or sub-regional boundaries. Indeed, the consultative brief that accompanied the circular letter made a point of suggesting the importance of *identity*; that the network should mean something to the learners who might engage with it.

A readily understood identity and accessibility are likely to be of importance to learners. Although generalisations are dangerous, many vocational learners will be able to satisfy their needs at institutions they can reasonably travel to from home. In the longer run a more comprehensive national system rooted in easily transferable credit is clearly desirable. There are dangers associated with local initiatives and a diversity of models, but we have to start somewhere. There is no real opportunity to launch a 'national scheme' outside particular specialist subjects. Progress will require close engagement of partners, working out the details of provision for learners. As networks are established there will be a need for mechanisms to link them so that they can learn from one another, and so that local developments are shaped with an eye to generalising the lessons from particular experiences.

A focus on learners

It is still early days in developing lifelong learning networks. One way of understanding how they might develop is to ask a series of central questions focused on the learner.

Is the proposed network clear about 'who are the learners' and 'which are the learning programmes' that the network will target?

Not all vocational learners have the same needs. Apprentices in different occupational areas may have widely different learning experiences, with some much more ready to tackle HE than others. For some apprentices the task will be to establish the contact and support that leads to HE entry after a period in employment. BTEC or AVCE students have followed programmes more clearly designed for HE entry. The question for these students may be the range of programmes and institutions they can actually access, and the appropriateness of the teaching and learning styles they will encounter. For students already in HE, studying higher national qualifications or a Foundation Degree, the issues will centre around the availability of clear progression opportunities to honours degrees, continuing professional development (CPD) and other postgraduate study.

How can existing progression opportunities for these learners in respect of these programmes be improved?

The first task for any network is a review of existing progression opportunities. The first proposals for lifelong learning networks are much stronger on initial access for new work-based learners than they are on how the experience of those already engaged in vocational learning can be improved. There is almost a blindness to vocational learners already in the system. Yet the experience of these learners is central. It is possible to enhance access without improving progression.

What further curriculum innovation and development, and changes in learning and teaching styles, are required to facilitate progression for these learners?

Much might be achieved by changing the way the existing curriculum is accessed and the way it is delivered. But the different experience of vocational learners will present challenges for HE, particularly in providing appropriate higher learning for those with competence-based qualifications (HEQC 1995). Partners in the network may need to provide bridging courses or other forms of learning support to enable learners to access HE programmes, or new programmes to provide alternative progression routes. Some networks, for example, are exploring the possibility of developing work-based top-up (honours) degrees for Foundation Degree graduates.

What mechanism will the network deploy to ensure that these learners can move from one programme to another and from one institution to another?

In many ways this is the key question: what commitments will partners enter into that will guarantee progression for vocational learners? Potential networks are likely to establish a *'progression accord'* based on agreement for credit accumulation and transfer, and this is a feature of early proposals. This will have to take account of existing credit accumulation and transfer (CAT) initiatives to ensure compatibility with national and European developments in this area.

How will learners be able to engage and re-engage with learning over a lifetime, and how will institutions facilitate this re-engagement?

If networks provide the advice and guidance needed, the *'negotiated learning'* of personalised learning programmes, learners will be able to build on prior learning but also take advantage of new, and perhaps quite different, opportunities that may be more appropriate as their lives and careers develop. The key will be to develop the mechanisms that keep learners in touch with the network.

Conclusion

Lifelong learning networks will challenge the marginal status of vocational learners, connect HE to the skills agenda, encourage progression from FE to HE, link colleges with HEIs, and sustain critical connections between HEIs in a more differentiated sector.

References

Ainley, P. (1993) Class and Skill: Changing Divisions of Knowledge and Skill. London: Cassell Educational.

Gospel, H. (1994) 'The survival of apprenticeship training: a British, American, Australian comparison', *British Journal of Industrial Relations* 32.4, pp. 505–22.

Greenwood, Maggie, Gareth Parry, and others (2002) *Progression from HNC/Ds to Honours Degrees: Diversity, Complexity and Change*. London: LSDA (Learning and Skills Development Agency) in association with the School of Education, University of Sheffield.

Higher Education Quality Council (HEQC) (1995) *Vocational Qualifications and Standards*. London: HEQC.

Keeble, S. P. (1992) *The Ability to Manage: A Study of British Management 1890–1990*. Manchester: Manchester University Press.

Little, Brenda, with Helen Connor, Yann Lebeau, David Pierce, Elaine Sinclair, Liz Thomas and Karen Yarrow (2000) *Vocational Higher Education: Does It Meet Employers' Needs?* London: LSDA.

McKinlay, A. (1991) 'A certain shortsightedness: metalworking, innovation and apprenticeship 1997–1939', in H. Gospel (ed.), *Industrial Training and Technological Innovation*. London: Routledge.

Oliver, J. M., and J. R. Turton (1982) 'Is there a shortage of skilled labour?' *British Journal of Industrial Relations* 20.2, pp. 195–200.

Owen, G. (1991) *From Empire to Europe*. London: HarperCollins.

Pagnamenta, P., and R. Overy (1984) *All Our Working Lives*. London: BBC.

Parry, G., P. Davies and J. Williams (2003) *Dimensions of Difference: Higher Education in the Learning and Skills Sector*. London: LSDA.

Pollard, S. (1989) *Britain's Prime and Britain's Decline*. London: Edward Arnold.

Sanderson, M. (1972). *The Universities and British Industry 1850–1970*. London: Routledge & Kegan Paul.

Sanderson, M. (1988) 'Education and economic decline: 1890 to the 1980s', *Oxford Review of Economic Policy* 4, pp. 38–50.

Wolf, Alison (2002) *Does Education Really Matter?* London: Penguin.

CHAPTER ELEVEN

Tertiary education: A Scottish perspective[1]

Laurence Howells

Introduction

The purpose of this chapter is to sketch out some of the lines along which tertiary education might develop in Scotland.

The context is the publishing of the Bill to merge the Scottish Further and Higher Education Funding Councils. A key element of the Bill is the requirement to secure a coherent system of further and higher education. This chapter suggests some ways that learners, employers and economic development agencies, government and the new funding council might take this agenda forward together.

Context

Scotland has been successful in creating high demand for learning and high quality provision. We have high participation rates. For example in 2001 over 50 per cent of young Scots were participating in higher education (HE). There is evidence of demand for non-advanced further education outstripping supply. Nearly all colleges are meeting or exceeding their student number targets, and colleges across the whole of Scotland are reporting greater need to prioritise the groups that they recruit and select for some courses. The results of external quality assessment of teaching and learning show consistently high quality results. Employer and student surveys show high levels of satisfaction with what is being delivered.

However, there are issues which need to be addressed, all of which are the result of complex factors. For example, participation is skewed by social class in Higher Education Institutions (HEIs) and by geography. Retention and achievement rates are slightly lower than in the rest of the UK. While Higher National (HN) qualifications are primarily stand-alone qualifications in their own right, they are increasingly being seen also as progression routes to degree-level education, but concerns have been expressed about the effectiveness of these routes, though the evidence is not fully clear. Scotland has consistently performed less well than the rest of the UK economically, showing a dependence on the public sector, low business birth rates and low investment in research, development and innovation.

Further and higher education is currently funded by two Funding Councils, which are supported by a single executive. Earlier in 2004 the Scottish Executive introduced a draft Bill to the Scottish Parliament the Tertiary Education (Funding etc.) (Scotland) Bill, essentially to merge the two Funding Councils. A key duty under the draft Bill was to 'secure the adequate and efficient provision of tertiary education'. Various aspects of the Bill were criticised in the course of the subsequent consultation, with concerns ranging from the autonomy of institutions, to excessive central planning powers. Particularly relevant to this discussion were concerns about the meaning and implications of the word 'tertiary' for academic structures, funding levels and diversity of institutions and provision.

The revised Further and Higher Education (Scotland) Bill as laid before the Scottish Parliament avoids the term 'tertiary'. The duties section has been amended and substitutes a duty to secure 'coherent provision' by institutions as a whole of high-quality further and higher education.

There is a very consensual mood over education in Scotland at the moment – an example being the highly effective way in which the Scottish Executive handled the consultation and redrafting of the above Bill. This gives us the opportunity to build a more coherent system, because we have the basis for people to speak together. Recent examples include: the way that quality assessment/enhancement has developed in Scotland in a partnership between institutions, NUS (the National Union of Students) (Scotland), the quality assurance agencies and the funding councils; the joint working that happens between schools, further education colleges (FECs) and higher education institutions (HEIs) on widening access; and increasingly effective working between government, the funding councils, the institutions, the qualifications authority, and enterprise bodies on economic and social justice agendas. Partly, this has been achieved through the size and scale of Scotland and its education system – (20 HEIs, 47 FE colleges, a population of 5 million) – enabling such dialogue; but also, though more needs to be done here, through broad agreement about purposes and roles.

This chapter explores what the implications of this might be for the future development of further and higher education in Scotland.

Coherence – planning

If the Bill is passed as drafted, the new Council will have to be more explicit in its thinking about what *coherence* might mean for the pattern of provision and of institutions. We will probably need to think about provision from two perspectives: from the learner perspective, what would coherent provision look like from a learners' point of view, and from the perspective of the economy and society, are the patterns optimal?

But we probably need also to think about what are the forces that create the patterns that we observe and how they operate before we then jump to the conclusion that we should be acting to change things. We believe there is advantage in thinking about the operation of the learning 'market' from a systems perspective, starting with the assumption that the primary things that drive the patterns of provision are the choices that learners make.

This is a huge simplification. But at the end of the day it is true that if learners do not turn up for a programme it will close. And learners' choices are influenced by what they perceive the outcomes are likely to be for them, in particular, and increasingly, by what learners think the employment outcomes are likely to be. This means that institutions have to listen to what learners and employers are saying, and adapt what they do.

This leads to the idea that we should focus on actions which make this system work more effectively, by shifting our focus onto helping learners make more informed choices and employers influence provision more effectively, rather than seeking to solve problems by seeking directly to plan institutions' provision. Also, perhaps, this suggests that coherence will be more about a continuing process rather than a defined state or end-point. We should be trying to engineer circumstances that are likely to lead to institutions' outputs cohering, without necessarily trying to over-specify what good coherence might look like at any particular time, and in the expectation that this will in any case change.

Coherence – (necessarily) merger/rationalisation/collaboration

It is striking how differently provision is organised in different parts of Scotland. From an administrative perspective it might seem tidy to look for mergers and rationalisation between institutions. The obvious case could be Glasgow, where there are ten FECs, five HEIs and a population of about 1 million, depending where you draw the boundary. It is argued that things would be better if there were fewer institutions or more city-wide coordination of provision. And things are beginning to change, with some mergers taking place or being considered.

In fact there has been more tertiary collaborative activity in the rural parts of Scotland with initiatives such as the University of the Highlands and Islands (UHI) Millennium Institute – a collaboration between eight FECs and a number of other academic partners – delivering higher education across the Highlands region, and with aspirations to become a university in its own right. The Crichton campus in Dumfries in the South-West is a collaboration between four HEIs and FECs aiming to bring higher education to a rural area with particularly low participation rates. A similar collaboration between Heriot-Watt University and Borders College is being explored in the South-East at Galashiels.

These examples of tertiary collaboration illustrate a truism which is that *sustainable* collaboration is driven only by a real need and real benefits to all the partners. Intrinsic needs of the business or the market – in these cases associated with issues of small-scale, sparse populations and distance – are powerful drivers. We need to be wary of extrinsic factors or external drivers, and of assumptions of administrative tidiness.

That is not to say that we should not be creating an environment which encourages and is benign to cooperation, but we should be careful not to drive a collaborative agenda too hard. And we should be looking at a wider range of models of collaboration, not simply equating this with restructuring. A particularly important area of collaboration between parts of the system in Scotland is likely to be the opportunity to redesign Higher National qualifications (delivered by FE colleges and validated by the Scottish Qualification Authority) with an eye on the structure of university qualifications – to design-in easier articulation routes for learners with maximum credit for prior learning. This sort of coherence is very different from, and arguably much more important to learners than, what you might call the 'administrative' coherence associated with restructuring of the provider network.

A particularly fruitful area for collaboration in the new environment in Scotland is likely to be between tertiary education and the enterprise community. Maybe we need to substitute a new word for *collaboration* here? I suggest we should be thinking more about *alignment* – of goals, of values and of outcomes – than collaboration. Where organisations have different functions but we want them to cohere in what they do, alignment may be a more fruitful way forward. *Collaboration* too often becomes an end in itself, with organisations trying to find things to do together for the sake of it, and thereby finding themselves straying onto each other's territory – exactly the opposite outcome to what we were seeking.

Coherence – everything is the same

Coherence does not mean that everything should be the same. In fact we are seeking more individualisation of provision. We are seeking greater recognition that different learners have different styles and needs, and a more customised response from institutions to them. We are seeking provision that helps learners become more creative and entrepreneurial. We are seeking a system that responds more rapidly to changes in the economy.

The same applies to institutions. We want institutions to be unique, special. Institutions and places and regions have different characters and needs. We know that where they have a choice groups of learners with different characteristics cluster in institutions of particular character, and by doing so play a part in reinforcing and reinventing their character. We want institutions to vie with each other, to be ambitious, vibrant and outstanding. We want the system as a whole to provide a huge range of opportunities – basic literacy and numeracy, craft training, academic study, medicine, nursing, research, and so on.

So coherence has to mean something about allowing these different pieces of the jigsaw to have a life of their own, but somehow fit together.

So how could we make this all fit together?

A possible way forward might be to start with *vision and values*, where we would probably quite quickly find common ground about the purposes and goals of tertiary education: around helping people improve their life chances; around helping learners develop the skills, attributes and knowledge that will make them employable; around high quality and around social justice; around cultural awareness, values and people's ability to make ethical judgements.

We then might think about the *systemic structures* that we need to deliver that kind of vision. These might include: joined-up qualifications; a better understanding of learning and what practices promote good learning in what circumstances; common principles and values for how we treat learners; more readily available information about provision; better ways of listening to learners and listening to employers; partnerships between institutions, communities, enterprise organisations, etc; joined-up funding structures and systems.

We then might reflect on the *patterns we see in society* and target action at these areas: for example, patterns of deprivation, participation and achievement, outcomes from individual institutions, courses and programmes. But we should celebrate and encourage institutions and programmes in being different and responding to different segments of the 'market'. Where this 'market' is not working well we should consider how to make it work better.

But we must treat *individuals as individuals*. We should not assume that particular forms of education are necessarily right for everyone. We should be seeking the best next step for each learner.

Possible actions

This suggests that coherent tertiary education might emerge from working on a common vision, with points of commonality between different institutions tackling different parts of the market. Possible actions that might contribute to this would be:

- Stimulating discussion with stakeholders about the values, purposes and vision of the education system. A practical example is the work just published by the Scottish Funding Councils for Further and Higher Education on employability, *Learning to Work* (SFCFHE 2004).
- Investing in joining-up qualifications at the point at which they are designed. As a practical example, the Scottish Qualification Authority in partnership with the Colleges is modernising its HN portfolio. This is an ideal opportunity to include in the design rules 'joining up' with degree-level qualifications.[2] We should also expect HEIs to consider how they join up with HN qualifications when approving and revising degree programmes.

- Investing in common understanding of what research tells us about learning and its implications for teaching, assessment and curriculum design. This is not to say that there is only one way of teaching that works – precisely the opposite – but in a joined-up system we would expect to have a shared evidence-based view of how to support learning that is appropriate for particular learners and for particular circumstances, and a better understanding of the problematical relationship between teaching and learning; what is taught is not (necessarily) what is learnt. We would expect reflection on this evidence and on our own practices and its outcomes. We would also expect learning from each other about our practices. As a practical example, in Scotland we are thinking about how these ideas could be taken forward through our approach to quality enhancement themes across the whole of tertiary education (SFCFHE 2003a).
- Invest in helping learners to make better choices, founding this on the principle that we should be seeking the *best next step for an individual*. This includes much more than simply providing better information, it requires learners and their influencers to be equipped to reflect on themselves and to evaluate information. A practical example is the *careers planning journey* tool being promoted by Careers Scotland (Careers Scotland).
- Trying to ensure that learner support or other funding policies do not distort learner choices inappropriately. The Scottish Executive's review of funding for learners should address this. There will remain a challenge for the new merged Funding Council to think about and justify its approaches to its funding methods.
- Try to be much more consistent in valuing equal but different routes that learners take through their education and lives. In particular, government should continually emphasise the idea that excellence in provision of education should be defined as optimising value added for the learner. We know that we cannot avoid other parts of society using other, sometimes elitist, value systems; government should press this idea, since no-one else will. A practical example is the decision in Scotland to try to avoid being perceived as defining excellence of learning and teaching in HEIs in terms of, for example, entry qualifications (SFCFHE 2003b).

Dangers

There are significant dangers. Arguments about funding and funding levels could fracture the consensus. This could become particularly pointed as demographic changes begin to bite. There will be a significant drop in the number of young Scots towards the end of the decade and the Scottish population has been gradually declining for many years. The impact of enlarging the European Union, and top-up fees in England, could have unpredictable effects on student behaviour and on institutional responses. Such changes could damage the development of coherent tertiary education, pushing people to focus back on their place in the hierarchy of institutions and building barriers to keep others out.

We need to be aware of such dangers and act carefully to create the environment for institutions to peacefully coexist, to be different and successful, to be comfortable with where they are and what they do, but still to keep optimising value-added for learners at the core of developing policy.

Conclusion

Perhaps paradoxically, having dropped the term *tertiary* from the Bill to merge the Funding Council, in Scotland we stand a better chance of creating something that from the point of view of the learner is more coherent and more joined up than ever before. Crucial to achieving this will be thinking about the term *coherent*, and finding mechanisms at several different levels to make such coherence a reality.

Building on and maintaining a consensus on values, purposes and goals among the key stakeholders – learners, employers, institutions and government – will be crucial. The way that the Scottish Executive handled and responded to the consultation on the merger Bill has reinforced and helped to create a very positive atmosphere for these discussions.

Notes

1   Laurence Howells writes in a personal capacity. These views do not necessarily represent those of the Scottish Funding Councils for further and higher education.

2   The work of the Scottish Credit and Qualifications Framework on mapping, tracking and bridging between colleges and universities is of interest here. See http://college2uni.scqf.org.uk/college2uni/mapping.aspx

References

Careers Scotland, *Careers Planning Continuum*, http://www.careers-scotland.org.uk

SFCFHE (Scottish Funding Councils for Further and Higher Education) (2003a) *Update on Quality Enhancement Themes*, CL HE/45/03. Edinburgh: SFCFHE.

SFCFHE (Scottish Funding Councils for Further and Higher Education) (2003b) *An Enhancement-Led Approach to Quality Assurance: Progress Report*, CL HE/04/03. Edinburgh: SFCFHE. Available online at http://www.shefc.ac.uk/library/06854fc203db2fbd000000f43505069e/he0403.htmlpublic

SFCFHE (Scottish Funding Councils for Further and Higher Education) (2004) *Learning to Work*. Edinburgh: SFCFHE.

The Scottish Parliament (2004) *Further and Higher Education (Scotland) Bill*. Available online at http://www.scottish.parliament.uk/business/bills/billsInProgress/furtherEd.htm

CHAPTER TWELVE

Why the English are different

Gareth Parry

England, like the other countries of the United Kingdom, achieved mass levels of participation in higher education on the basis of a dual system of post-secondary education. Contrary to the expectations of some commentators, the division of this system into two discrete sectors, one for institutions of higher education and one for establishments of further education, proved neither a brake on expansion nor a barrier to collaboration. Nevertheless, the fitness of these arrangements has come under increased scrutiny in the post-devolution period, with Scotland choosing to merge its funding bodies for tertiary education and England reaffirming its commitment to separate sectors and parallel agencies.

To an extent not found in the other home countries, England has been untaken by concepts of tertiary education, especially those that bring higher and further education into a common planning or funding framework. Whether in the early separation made between autonomous universities and local authority further education or, after 1988, the ternary structure of university, polytechnic and further education or, after 1992, the return to a dual set of post-secondary arrangements, the need to segment and stratify institutions by sector has been a powerful element in English policy-making. While Scotland, Wales and Northern Ireland have inherited the same divisions or operated similar demarcations, these jurisdictions have generally been more at ease with tertiary notions. Indeed, following administrative and then political devolution, each has sought closer coordination and joint working between its higher and further education bodies.

In England, the movement has if anything been in the opposite direction. Despite joint initiatives to support partnerships between higher and further education and, most recently, a joint strategy to advance vocational progression into and through higher education, sector remits and preoccupations have intensified. Why have successive reforms reproduced and reinforced sector divisions at a time when policies for lifelong learning and widening participation might be expected to render these categories insensible or redundant? Why has tertiary thinking proved so difficult and dissonant in the English context? Or, from another angle, what made sector solutions so normal, durable and adaptable under English conditions?

No comprehensive examination of these questions can be offered here. Rather, a reminder is given of the contemporary history of post-secondary sectors and, drawing on selective 'home international' comparisons (Raffe 2000), a preliminary attempt is made to explain the salience of dual policy and regulatory regimes in the English context. The Englishness of these attachments is illustrated by comparison with Scotland in particular, with relevant reference to the situation in Wales and Northern Ireland. Apart from the smallness of these other systems, the intimacy of their policy communities, and the advantages of 'policy-practice proximity' (Griffiths 2003), attention is drawn here to distinctive features of the English encounter with mass higher education that continue to favour separation over integration. Finally, the strength and survival of sector structures in England is assessed in the light of policies intended to secure distinct provision for young people and specialist vocational provision in general further education colleges.

From a binary to a dual system

One indicator of the acceptance of sector differentiation in England was the infrequency and, when volunteered, the brevity of policy statements to justify these separations. One exception was the binary policy of the 1960s which, in creating a non-university sector of higher education, required a formal rejection of the Robbins recommendations. More significant for present-day arrangements however was the way that a distinction previously applied to the level of work undertaken in local authority colleges became the basis for distinguishing between institutions of higher education and establishments of further education, and for organising and administering them in separate sectors.

As a result of the rationalisation of teacher education in the 1970s and repeated efforts by central government to concentrate higher education in the strongest institutions, three 'tiers' of institutions began to emerge on the local authority side of the binary line. The polytechnics and the colleges of higher education constituted the first and second tiers respectively, each with a majority of their courses comprising 'advanced further education'. A third tier of colleges of further education, where most of the provision was 'non-advanced further education', offered courses of vocational higher education, mainly at levels below the first degree.

By the end of the 1970s there were still more than 300 colleges of further education in England with a stake in higher education, albeit usually a small one. According to the Oakes committee (Oakes 1978) set up to consider reform of the framework of higher education in the local authority sector, there were institutions (like the polytechnics) doing more than 90 per cent advanced work, others (including the colleges of higher education) with between 30 per cent and 90 per cent of provision at this level, and those – essentially the colleges of further education – doing less than 30 per cent advanced work. As well, there were a significant number of further education establishments that offered no advanced courses.

While the different balance of higher and lower-level work in individual institutions was usually apparent to those who needed to know, the ownership and control of the polytechnics and colleges by the local authorities ensured that the intermixture of advanced and non-advanced further education was preserved in the great majority of establishments. That link and the long-standing concern for the 'seamless robe' of further education was finally broken by the Education Reform Act of 1988 which removed the 29 English polytechnics and the larger colleges engaged predominantly in higher education from local government control. These institutions were transferred to a new Polytechnics and Colleges Funding Council (PCFC) and re-established as free-standing corporations. At the same time, the universities were transferred to a new Universities Funding Council.

The creation of these two funding councils maintained the binary line in higher education but, in terms of the larger post-secondary system, the more significant outcome of these reforms was the separation – structural and operational – maintained henceforth between 'institutions of higher education' (as they were now collectively described) and colleges of further education whose 'main concern' was work at the upper secondary and associated levels. With delegated powers, the colleges were to remain with local government and their remaining higher education work was to be funded in two ways. For their 'prescribed' higher education (postgraduate, first degree and full-time higher national diploma and equivalent courses) they would be funded by the PCFC. For their 'non-prescribed' higher education (part-time sub-degree provision, including higher national certificate courses) they would be funded through the local authorities.

As the accompanying White Paper made clear, not only was the local authority interest in higher education now regarded as 'residual' but the development of non-prescribed higher education in the local authority colleges would 'no longer be guided by a central planning agency' (DES 1987). Under the National Advisory Body for Local Authority Higher Education, a planning and funding authority for advanced further education established in 1982, all levels and modes of higher education came under a single national body (in which the local authority interest in higher education was retained). This body was abolished by the 1988 Act and, as a mark of the lesser or marginal importance attached to higher education in further education, responsibility for this provision was split between central and local authorities.

In a pattern to be repeated in later years, it was left to the representative of a higher education body to outline the benefits that separation would bring to the redefined further education sector. The reforms, suggested the newly appointed Chief Executive of the PCFC, returned the name 'further education' to the sector: 'a name that is honourable and traditional and important' and one that was no longer burdened with the negative language of non-advanced further education. Relieved of the responsibility for higher education institutions and for courses of prescribed higher education, it made the mission for further education 'more prominent and more distinct' (Stubbs 1988).

The 1988 legislation was just the prelude to the full elaboration of a dual system in which a higher education sector and a further education or 'post-16 learning' sector would supersede earlier binary and ternary divisions. Following the Further and Higher Education Act of 1992, the further education colleges in turn were taken out of local authority control and, joined by the sixth form colleges (previously under schools regulations), both sets of institutions were incorporated into a new further education sector with its own funding council and inspectorate. The same Act abolished the binary line, enabled the polytechnics and some other establishments to adopt university titles, and established a single funding body for a new unified higher education sector.

These proposals were carried in separate White Papers and, mostly concerned with the composition and organisation of their respective sectors, neither document found it necessary to supply a rationale for the educational and institutional division of labour underpinning these dual arrangements. Furthermore, though the 1992 legislation allowed the Further Education Funding Council (FEFC) and the Higher Education Funding Council for England (HEFCE) to 'exercise jointly any of their functions', no expectation or duty was placed on the two bodies to integrate or harmonise their activities. The normal presumption was that they would communicate and consult with each other on a regular basis.

Organisational and relational matters were considered however by the national committee of inquiry into higher education (the Dearing committee 1996–97). Indeed, it was this inquiry which proposed that further education colleges in England take a leading role in the future expansion of higher education at the sub-degree levels and, in support of this 'special mission', that all such provision should be funded directly by the HEFCE. It was recognised that these and related recommendations posed wide-ranging strategic questions: first, about the need for separate funding councils for higher and further education; and, second, about how funding responsibilities should be divided between them.

For England, the view taken by the Dearing inquiry was that a single funding body would be 'too large to work properly or to represent the range of interests adequately'. Given the scale of higher and further education in that country, and the need for a funding body to relate effectively to a large number of institutions, the inquiry recommended that separate funding councils for each sector should continue, with 'stronger arrangements for liaison at regional level, particularly to assist in widening participation' (NCIHE 1997). A specific outcome of this recommendation was a regionally based pro-gramme of widening participation projects, modestly funded by HEFCE and the FEFC (and its successor body) and jointly administered by the two councils (HEFCE 2003).

As for the funding responsibilities of these bodies, two main options were put to the committee. In the first, all sub-degree provision in the colleges would be funded by the further education finding body and all provision in higher education institutions (along with degree-level work in the colleges) funded by the higher education funding body. In the second option, the one 'closest to the current English model', all higher education, irrespective of its location, would be funded by the higher education funding authority. While the Scottish committee within the Dearing inquiry supported the former option for Scotland, the main inquiry committee favoured the latter option for England (and Wales) since:

only this could force a consideration of the relative costs of similar provision across all the providing institutions, be they in the further or higher education sector; that this would place enhanced responsibility for funding sub-degree provision squarely alongside that for other higher education; that it would not confuse delivery of sub-degree higher education with the remaining legal duty for further education of the Further Education Funding Councils; that it would be essentially a tidying-up of the current arrangements; and that the development of the sort of sub-degree qualifications with value . . . could only be achieved within the higher education context. (NCIHE 1997, 355)

Accordingly, the committee recommended that, in England and Wales, the funding for higher education, wherever delivered, should flow through the higher education funding body. In Scotland and Northern Ireland, on the other hand, the committee respected the preference expressed for the first option.

Viewed from a tertiary perspective, what was interesting about these preferences, and about the proposal to develop higher education in the colleges, was the need for the Dearing inquiry to range more widely than originally intended. At the outset, the committee chose to resist any broadening of the scope of its studies to embrace 'tertiary' education: 'we had to set some boundaries' and 'we already faced an enormous task'. In the absence of a parallel inquiry into the future of further education, or a strong evidence base referenced to the world of colleges, this self-denying ordinance was always likely to create some difficulty for the committee if, as happened, it made key recommendations addressed to another sector.

That no dialogue was maintained with the Kennedy committee (1994–97), an inquiry into widening participation in further education set up by the FEFC, was another illustration of the play, power and observance of sector boundaries. Notwithstanding its original remit, the Kennedy committee reported more broadly on the nature and purpose of education in the college sector and, like the Dearing report, its recommendations were accorded a full and formal government response in a Green Paper on lifelong learning published in 1998.

If Dearing offered one kind of justification for the value of two funding bodies, it was not until a White Paper in 1999 that a reform proposal aimed at England tackled the case for separating higher education from the rest of the post-secondary system. Described by the Secretary of State as 'the most significant and far reaching reform ever enacted to post-16 learning in this country', the White Paper *Learning to Succeed* (DfEE 1999) proposed the establishment of a new body – the Learning and Skills Council (LSC) – to take responsibility for the strategic development, planning, funding, management and quality assurance for post-16 learning 'excluding higher education'.

Under this reform, the LSC assumed funding responsibility for further education sector colleges (from the FEFC), for school sixth forms (from the local education authorities), for government-funded training and workforce development (from the training and enterprise councils), and for adult and community learning (from local government). Advised by two committees, one for young people and one for adult learners, the national LSC was to operate through a network of local LSCs that would plan and coordinate provision locally.

These structural changes, seen as essential to bring greater coherence, coordination and responsiveness to the new post-16 sector, were not extended to higher education. Two reasons were given for not giving the LSC direct funding responsibility for provision at the higher levels. The first involved a claim to the uniqueness of higher education: its contribution was international and national as well as regional and local. Although universities should be responsive to the needs of local employers and business, both to meet skills requirements and the application of research, they also 'operate on a wider stage and require a different approach to funding'. The second justification was more operational: to include higher education would under-mine one of the main aims of the reform, which was to 'bring order to an area which is overly complex'. Broadening this remit to include higher education would, it was stated, 'complicate' this remit significantly.

In a manner similar to that governing the previous relationship between the FEFC and the HEFCE, the national Learning and Skills Council would need to:

> *take full account of the contribution and potential of this important sector and will work with the Higher Education Funding Council for England and the HE institutions to achieve the National Learning Target for Level 4 (first degree or equivalent). (DfEE 1999, 42)*

Equally, there was no reason why the exclusion and separation of higher education from the funding of colleges, sixth forms, training providers and adult education centres should deter collaboration or progression:

> *Ensuring that there is seamless transition through learning so that everyone is able to progress to the highest level possible will be key. There is particular scope for collaborative activities and sharing facilities between universities and FE colleges, and for adult continuing education. We want to increase further the number of people who combine study with work, particularly in the 18–30 age group and technician levels. (ibid.)*

Since the passage of the Learning and Skills Act in 2000, the two funding councils have been asked to attend to any barriers that stand in the way of smooth progression and effective partnership at the interface of the post-16 sector and higher education. For the state and its agencies, there was no contradiction between dual structures and the capacity of the system to link its sectors, providers and programmes in responsive, efficient and flexible ways.

From elite to mass to universal access within a dual system

As a result of the 1988, 1992 and 2000 reforms, the English evolved structures, procedures and policies that reinforced a dual conception and ordering of education beyond the compulsory phase. At the same time, these arrangements proved no disincentive to higher education institutions and further education establishments entering into collaborative relationships of increasing variety. More significantly, it was over this same period that the four countries in the United Kingdom, led by Scotland and Northern Ireland, saw much larger numbers and proportions of their population enter higher education (Parry 2005).

If policy in England was marked by a deepening attachment to dualism, more distinctive again was the means by which that country accomplished the breakthrough to mass higher education. The English road to mass higher education diverged from that in the other home countries, Scotland in particular, both in terms of the pace and pattern of growth as well as the institutions that took most of this expansion. Moreover, having achieved a near doubling of the full-time participation rate for young people between 1988 and 1994, largely on the basis of entry to first-degree courses at establishments of higher education, the English chose to embark on another phase of undergraduate growth based on a quite different set of qualifications, institutions and sectors. As in the earlier shift from an extended elite to a mass scale of higher education, the subsequent drive to near universal access by the end of the present decade presupposed no major change to the system architecture separating the further and higher education sectors.

Apart from differences in the history, size and complexity of their education systems, along with the impetus for policy review provided by political devolution, one of the other major reasons why arguments for unified or merged tertiary arrangements acquired so little purchase in England – in contrast to Scotland – had to do with the growth trajectory of English higher education. Put simply, with only a small fraction of its higher education remaining in the further education sector (a direct result of the 1988 changes) and as a consequence of the character of the spectacular expansion that followed, the college contribution to higher education in England was very different from that which gave force to proposals for tertiary reorganisation in Scotland.

During the peak years of growth, at the end of the 1980s and into the first half of the 1990s, participation in Scottish higher education grew faster in the colleges than in either the universities or the central institutions and colleges of education. By the turn of the century, around one in four higher education students in Scotland were enrolled in the further education sector, nearly all on one-year and two-year programmes of vocational higher education. In England, the picture was reversed (Table 12.1).

	1989/90		1993/94		2000/01	
England						
Higher education institutions	688.4		1044.2		1327.4	
Further education colleges	119.2	(15%)	146.4	(12%)	187.3	(12%)
Total	131.6		179.7		262.9	
Scotland						
Higher education institutions	98.5		132.5		190	
Further education colleges	33.1	(25%)	47.3	(26%)	72.9	(28%)
Total	47.2		73.6		102.5	
Wales						
Higher education institutions	45.6		72.5		93.6	
Further education colleges	1.6	(3%)	1.1	(1%)	8.9	(9%)
Total	47.2		73.6		102.5	
Northern Ireland						
Higher education institutions	23.8		32.6		42.8	
Further education colleges	3.4	(12%)	5.1	(14%)	12	(22%)
Total	27.3		37.7		54.8	
United Kingdom						
Higher education institutions	856.3		1281.8		1653.8	
Further education colleges	157.3	(16%)	199.9	(13%)	281.1	(155)
Total	1013.7		1481.6		1934.9	

Sources: Education and USR, Welsh Office.
Notes:
1. Figures for franchise
2. Account should not be

Table 12.1 Students undertaking higher education and higher-level qualifications by country and type of institution, excluding Open University (Thousands: percentage of higher education students in further education colleges in brackets)

Not only was the overall rate of expansion higher in England but – unlike north of the border – it was the establishments of higher education, the polytechnics in particular, that led the growth to mass levels of participation. Recruitment to higher education was slowest in the colleges of further education and, without the franchising of undergraduate teaching to colleges by the fast-expanding polytechnics, the decrease in the proportion of higher education in further education would have been even greater. Today, an estimated one in nine (12 per cent) of the higher education student population in England (excluding the Open University) is taught in further education settings. Fifteen years ago, at the beginning of the mass phase, this proportion was closer to one in seven, at 15 per cent of the total.

When, in devising its lifelong learning strategy, the Scottish Executive recommended merger of the funding bodies for further and higher education in Scotland, not only was there a substantial amount of higher education in the colleges but 50 per cent of young Scots were already participating in some kind of higher education (Scottish Executive 2003). Arguably, it was the significance and intersection of these two features that made discussion of this measure necessary and, in the circumstances of devolution, timely. In England, the size and balance of activity on these two fronts was always unlikely, on its own, to trigger serious consideration of tertiary integration.

There were more immediate reasons as well why unified post-secondary arrangements were off the agenda in England. The recency of the Learning and Skills Act, which had sanctioned sector partition only four years earlier, made it politically impossible for alternative models to enter into public debate, at least in the short term. Not even the critiques of 'sectorism' mounted by those close to the governing party – for example, Wagner (1998) and Piatt and Robinson (2001) – were sufficient to encourage larger ambitions. On the contrary, the Government was more than willing to admit that it had enough on its hands in sorting out the post-16 education and training sector, rather than inviting yet more difficulty. Better to keep higher education, the sector with less serious problems, at a distance from this priority zone.

That tertiary questions rarely impinged on the assumptive worlds of English policy-makers was a tribute to the strength of sector boundaries, identities and cultures. Even after the Government had accepted the Dearing recommendations to expand sub-degree higher education in the colleges, neither the transfer of funding responsibility to HEFCE for all higher education (save for some higher-level vocational qualifications that remained in the category of non-prescribed higher education) nor the need for the funding council to deal with many more colleges than previously, were sufficient to raise questions about the appropriateness of sector regimes (Parry and Thompson 2002).

The modest scale of higher education in English further education was a major but not the only factor explaining why future access and growth policies were expected to be achieved and accommodated within existing structures. In contrast to Scotland, where higher certificate and diploma courses in the colleges were a discrete segment or 'parallel system' of higher education (Gallacher 2002), one of the legacies of the lurch to mass higher education in England was that further education colleges and higher education institutions continued to pursue a shared mission in respect of sub-degree higher education. At the same time, higher education in further education became more dispersed and disparate, with the great majority of colleges possessing small amounts of provision and, as before, some with no higher education at all.

Short-cycle vocational qualifications in Scotland were largely the preserve of further education colleges and they were directly funded – first by the Scottish Office and then by their own funding body – to pursue this mission. It was markedly different in England: the higher national diploma and certificate were offered by institutions in both sectors; the further education colleges were funded directly and indirectly for their higher education; and their higher education and higher-level qualifications were awarded and quality assured by a range of bodies, including the universities.

Notwithstanding these overlapping territories, the higher education located in the English further education sector acquired 'a diversity and complexity all of its own' (Parry, Davies and Williams 2003). Based on two kinds of higher education (prescribed and non-prescribed) and two forms of funding (direct and indirect), college-delivered higher-level work comprised three sets of provision. First, and most numerous, were programmes of prescribed higher education funded directly by the HEFCE, assessed directly by the Quality

Assurance Agency for Higher Education (QAA), and offered by colleges in their own right.

The second set of programmes were also examples of prescribed higher education but they were funded through franchise agreements between higher education establishments and partner colleges. All or part of these courses were taught in college settings. Nevertheless, formal responsibility for the students and the quality and standards of the programmes rested with the higher education institution (as the organisation in receipt of HEFCE funding).

A phenomenon of the expansion years, franchising had brought new subjects and qualifications (including more at first-degree level) into college-based higher education. It also brought some colleges into higher education for the first time. According to a recent review of indirect funding arrangements in England, there were 75 higher education establishments and 298 further education colleges involved in franchise partnerships and HEFCE-recognised funding consortia. In other words, over half of the total of higher education institutions and around two-thirds of further education colleges were party to such arrangements. Franchise students accounted for nearly a third of all those taught on courses of prescribed higher education in the colleges. However, the funding passed to colleges to teach these students was less than that received for their own prescribed courses: a result of top-slicing by the franchising universities, at levels ranging from 5 per cent to 50 per cent (Parry, Moseley, Thompson and Blackie 2003).

The third area of higher education provision in further education was non-prescribed higher education. Funded mainly through the Learning and Skills Council, its description as higher education was disputed in some quarters. This work included higher-level professional, technical and vocational qualifications as well as provision leading to national vocational qualifications at levels 4 and 5.

In 2000/01, around 340 further education establishments delivered one or more of these three sorts of provision, much of it concentrated in some of the larger colleges and the remainder widely scattered. Indeed, just 57 colleges were responsible for half of the total number of students studying at these levels. Even so, most further education colleges offering higher education had students in each of the three categories.

Without the critical mass achieved by colleges – individually and collectively – in the Scottish system, and without their (now close to) exclusive responsibility for a specific set of qualifications, higher education in the college sector in England was at some disadvantage in the competition for students, resources and plaudits. Without the profile, cohesiveness, commonality and solidity of their Scottish counterparts, colleges were dependent on another sector, another funding council and, increasingly, another set of institutions (the universities) for their higher education. These were not conditions favourable to thinking and acting 'tertiary'.

Redundant, residual or functional?

As noted already, the British-cum-English preference has generally been for unification within sectors, not between higher education and the rest of the post-secondary system. Separate sectors of higher education, each with their own funding body since 1993, have been a common feature of the English, Scottish and Welsh systems. So far, only in Scotland will the funding councils for each sector be merged, but in that country and in Wales these two bodies already operated a joint executive. To an extent less achievable in England, they were able to build mutual understanding and, where appropriate, dovetail their approaches and processes. Prior to the suspension of the Northern Ireland Assembly, similar mechanisms were in place in that territory.

In England, especially after the 2000 Act and the bringing together of post-16 providers into a vast new learning and skills sector, the two sides of the dual system looked very different and, in some major respects, diverged in their roles and responsibilities. With more than 6 million 'learners' in the post-16 sector and approaching 2 million 'students' in the higher education sector, the LSC was unlikely to achieve the same depth of relationship with its more than 4,000 providers (including the further education colleges) as that managed by HEFCE in exercising responsibility for 'the overall health and development' of its 130 or so higher education establishments.

Whereas the funding council for higher education was keen to assert that it was not a planning body (steering was another matter), the LSC was set up as just that, with further education colleges and other providers having their core provision planned and coordinated locally, through 47 local LSCs. Furthermore, the reform of the post-16 sector involved a new system of targets and performance management, strategic area reviews to assess the pattern of provision in each part of the country, and collaborative working between colleges and schools across the 14 to 19 phase of learning.

Divergences were also apparent in the policies for each sector, such that further education colleges were expected to perform tasks that pulled in different and converse directions. Among the higher education policies applied to the post-16 sector were those envisaging a prominent role for colleges in the delivery of the foundation degree and, thereby, making an important contribution to the target set for 50 per cent of 18–30-year-olds to participate in higher education by the year 2010. The higher education mission of colleges had been reaffirmed in the 2003 White Paper on higher education (DfES 2003) yet no such policy figured strongly in *Success for All* (DfES 2002) – the quality improvement strategy for colleges – nor in the White Paper on skills (DfES *et al.* 2003), which had other priorities in mind for further education providers.

At the heart of policies directed at colleges by the central authorities outside the higher education sector, including the 14–19 phase, were those aimed at creating more differentiation between and within providers of upper secondary and further education. As an extension of its school choice policies, and in recognition that some types of establishment performed better than others in retaining and qualifying their students, the Blair Government urged further education colleges, sixth form colleges and schools to 'play to their strengths'.

Accordingly, individual further education colleges were pressed to demonstrate their distinctiveness and to cultivate a specialist focus: 'The need first and foremost for each college to identify what it is best at, and to make that field of excellence central to its mission.' By 2001, the first 16 'pathfinder' colleges had been announced and, by 2004, half of all general further education colleges were planned to have an established vocational specialism for which they were recognised as a centre of excellence. Although they had joined the further education sector in 1993 and some had diversified their courses, the sixth form colleges had maintained their focus on upper secondary academic qualifications. Given their delimited mission, more selective entry and the 'better' overall performance of their students in the main qualifications for entry to higher education, most sixth form colleges enjoyed a more secure position than many general further education colleges.

Furthermore, the government strategy on skills anticipated a specific role for the colleges in closing the 'skills gap' at the basic levels (especially for adults), in meeting regional and occupational needs at the intermediate levels (where the foundation degree was placed), and in taking some of the compulsory-age school population into their vocational courses (especially those benefiting least from the standard curriculum). Together with sixth form centres inside the college, these were some of the areas where further education establishments might develop 'distinct' provision for age-related groups.

At one end of this policy spectrum were programmes of higher education undertaken in partnership with universities and employers, operated under higher education regulations and requirements, and aimed at young and older adults. At the other were courses of further education run in association with schools, offered to those as young as 14 and 15, and likely to include pupils for whom school was a negative experience. Here was one set of policies intended to focus the work of colleges and another that would extend or stretch the mission of these institutions. Their origin, circulation and tension were testimony to a dual system.

For institutions funded by the LSC, judgements and recommendations about the appropriate pattern of provision in a given area were a matter for strategic area review. However, this planning exercise did not extend to institutions of higher education or to courses of prescribed higher education (such as the foundation degree) in further education colleges, whether funded directly or indirectly. Again, while strategic area review presupposed a capacity to plan, compose and develop such provision, the funding and steering of higher education in further education depended on managed markets.

Regional and labour market priorities, as interpreted by regional development agencies and a new band of sector skills councils, were among the criteria applied by the higher education funding body in allocating additional student numbers. Colleges and universities, on their own or (as preferred by government) in 'structured partnerships', bid for these funds in a highly competitive environment. Over and above these considerations was a concern about the quality of courses in a minority of colleges and about the risk of isolation posed by small pockets of higher education. The risk was likely to be greater, it was averred, where there was no link with a neighbouring higher education institution and where there was no anchoring in the core provision at the college.

Subject assessment by the QAA provided the higher education funding council with information about the standards of the programmes it funded in colleges. As the primary funder of colleges, with no remit for higher education, it was the planning and funding decisions of the LSC that were a crucial influence on the ability of these institutions to undertake higher-level work. One expression of these divided responsibilities, with implications for the quality and sustainability of higher education in further education, was the reluctance or refusal of the central authorities to take a view on whether some or all colleges should be engaged in such activity.

The join in these sector-led policies and processes, if there was one, lay in the desire of government to create 'a new vocational ladder' spanning secondary and post-secondary education (Blunkett 2001). At the upper end of this ladder, the foundation degree would provide a vocational route into higher education for those qualifying with upper secondary qualifications or through the award of credits for appropriate prior and work-based learning. At the lower end, more vocational versions of secondary qualifications were to be introduced for 14–16-year-olds that would open a pathway to more advanced programmes that were predominantly vocational or which combined academic and vocational study. Given the history and scope of its provision, the former further education sector was poised to supply vocational qualifications at each of the main levels in the new ladder. That purpose is still alive but not, it would seem, in the guise of the general further education college.

Instead of the eclipse of dual regimes and the collapse of sector identities, another prospect is the decline and eventual abandonment of further education as a category of institutions with family resemblances. What general, specialist, 'mixed economy' and sixth form colleges shared in common was loose and tenuous. The classifications retained by the further education funding bodies bore little relationship to function or usage, as in the definition of a small number of colleges as 'tertiary'. This survival from a previous era was a another reminder of the specificities and problems attached to tertiary language in the English case.

Whatever the disturbance or damage to further education traditions, a more segmented environment for academic, vocational and age-related education was even less likely to bring an end to rule by sector. The new traffic between schools and colleges, like the interface between universities and colleges, would carry some strains – notably about levels of funding, conditions of service, and salaries – but bring no necessary challenge to the authority of sectors.

Organisationally, what had been inhibited in the English post-secondary system was the development of dual-sector institutions where the further education component was large and significant enough to distinguish the mission, configuration and constituency of the university. The history of upward drift in the level and type of work conducted by institutions later accepted into higher education sector had, with one or two exceptions, allowed for no major presence of further education in their portfolio of courses. Interestingly, cross-sector mergers, the main vehicle for dual-sector establishments to come into being, produced few examples of this kind of organisation.

Finally, an argument can be made for the functional fit and convenience of dual sectors that is less do with controls on academic drift and more to do with structures that work to the overall advantage of institutions of higher education. The attempt to relieve further education of the burden of higher education, formalised in the 1988 Act and resisted by local government over many decades, was potentially undermined by the dramatic expansion of higher education that followed this reform. Unlike in Scotland, where central government continued to fund and foster a discrete, large and expanding share of higher education, no such division of academic labour was proposed in England. Instead, it was the sector bodies for higher education, not central government or further education, which exercised primary responsibility for the funding and quality assurance of the greater part of higher education.

Under these arrangements, colleges were still able to be funded directly for their prescribed higher education but, given that demand in England was strongest for the first degree at establishments of higher education, indirect funding became an increasingly important element in college-based higher education. During the post-1988 expansion, franchising to colleges was a means by which some of the fastest-growing polytechnics could increase and widen their recruitment even when capacity constraints had otherwise been reached. Similarly, when a policy of 'consolidation' was imposed on the system after 1994, the universities and colleges of higher education were able to review their franchise commitments and, where necessary, reduce or withdraw their involvement. In the classic manner, colleges were available to absorb some of the peaks of demand and, when circumstances changed, they were vulnerable to these franchise numbers being renegotiated and returned to the partner universities.

Dual divisions were not the main reason for weak demand for college-owned higher education, nor at the beginning was franchising anticipated or endorsed by the sector bodies. Nevertheless, their functional convenience for higher education institutions, always a much more powerful group than further education colleges, was readily acknowledged. Now, with indirect funding partnerships the preferred vehicle for colleges to grow their higher education, this more dependent relationship was inscribed into official policy. The betwixt and between status of higher education in further education, together with the weak branding and bargaining position of colleges, were features attributable to pursuit of sector interests and the asymmetries of power expressed in sector relationships.

These too were the structural constraints and conditions that shaped efforts to connect the two sectors, such as the much-vaunted proposal for 'partnerships for progression' (HEFCE and LSC 2001) and, as part of a joint progression strategy between the LSC and HEFCE, the development of 'lifelong learning networks' in individual regions (HEFCE and LSC 2004). Ahead of a partial deregulation of full-time fees for undergraduate education from 2006, the issue of dual policy and accountability in college-located higher education was likely to figure, in some shape or form, in the recently announced review into the role of further education colleges in England.

This was the first time in the history of further education that 'colleges' were the focus of an independent review set up at the request of the Blair administration. True to form, this would not be on the scale of a Robbins or a Dearing but, headed by the former chief executive of the Audit Commission for England and Wales (Sir Andrew Foster), it would take an independent look at 'the strategic positioning of the college sector'. Given that the 14–19 and skills strategies placed 'new and challenging demands on colleges', the review would aim:

> to identify the distinctive contribution colleges make to the learning and skills market, their long-term contribution to economic development and social inclusion and what more needs to happen to transform the sector. (DfES 2004)

No mention here of the higher education mission of colleges, let alone closer alignment of the two sectors, but a real opportunity perhaps to capture the tertiary moment.

References

Blunkett, D. (2001) *Education into Employability: The Role of the DfEE in the Economy.* London: Department for Education and Employment.

Department of Education and Science (1987) *Higher Education: Meeting the Challenge*, Cm. 114. London: The Stationery Office.

Department for Education and Employment (1999) *Learning to Succeed: A New Framework for Post-16 Learning*, Cm. 4392. London: The Stationery Office.

Department for Education and Skills (2002) *Success for All: Reforming Further Education and Training*, London: DfES.

Department for Education and Skills (2003) *The Future of Higher Education*, Cm. 5735. London: The Stationery Office.

Department for Education and Skills (2004) Letter from Charles Clarke and Chris Banks, 16 November 2004.

Department for Education and Skills, Department of Trade and Industry, Department of Work and Pensions and HM Treasury (2003) *21st Century Skills: Realising Our Potential: Individuals, Employers, Nation*, Cm. 5810. London: The Stationery Office.

Gallacher, J. (2002) 'Parallel lines? Higher education in Scotland's colleges and higher education institutions', *Scottish Affairs* 40, pp. 123–39.

Griffiths, M. (2003) 'Policy-practice proximity: the scope for college-based higher education and cross-sector collaboration in Wales', *Higher Education Quarterly* 57.4, pp. 355–75.

Higher Education Funding Council for England (2003) *Widening Participation Funded Projects: End of Programme Report*, 2003/40. Bristol: HEFCE.

Higher Education Funding Council for England and Learning and Skills Council (2001) *Partnerships for Progression: Proposals by the HEFCE and the Learning and Skills Council*, Consultation 01/73. Bristol: HEFCE.

Higher Education Funding Council for England and Learning and Skills Council (2004) *Lifelong Learning Networks*, Joint Letter from the Learning and Skills Council and HEFCE, LSC/AA000/1104/04 and HEFCE Circular Letter 12/2004, 3 June 2004.

National Committee of Inquiry into Higher Education (1997) *Higher Education in the Learning Society: Main report*. London: NCIHE.

Oakes, G. (1978) *Report of the Working Group on the Management of Higher Education in the Maintained Sector*. London: HMSO.

Parry, G. (2005) 'British higher education in the prism of devolution', in T. Tapper and D. Palfreyman (eds), *Understanding Mass Higher Education: Comparative Perspectives on Access*. Abingdon: RoutledgeFalmer.

Parry, G., and A. Thompson (2002) *Closer by Degrees: The Past, Present and Future of Higher Education in Further Education Colleges*. London: Learning and Skills Development Agency.

Parry, G., P. Davies and J. Williams (2003) *Dimensions of Difference: Higher Education in the Learning and Skills Sector*. London: Learning and Skills Development Agency.

Parry, G., R. Moseley, J. Thompson and P. Blackie (2003) *Review of Indirect Funding Agreements and Arrangements between Higher Education Institutions and Further Education Colleges*, Issues Paper 2003/57. Bristol: HEFCE.

Piatt, W., and P. Robinson (2001) *Opportunity for Whom? Options for the Funding and Structure of Post-16 Education*. London: Institute for Public Policy Research.

Raffe, D. (2000) 'Investigating the education systems of the United Kingdom', in D. Phillips (ed.), *The Education Systems of the United Kingdom*. Wallingford: Symposium Books.

Scottish Executive (2003) *Life through Learning. Learning through Life: The Lifelong Learning Strategy*. Edinburgh: Scottish Executive.

Stubbs, W. H. (1988) *The Polytechnics and Colleges Funding Council*, Speech to the Association of Colleges of Further and Higher Education, June 1988.

Wagner, L. (1998) *The Radical Implications of Lifelong Learning*, Philip Jones Memorial Lecture, 12 March 1998. Leicester: National Institute of Adult Continuing Education.

CHAPTER THIRTEEN

The tertiary moment?

David Watson

Introduction

As the author of the final chapter in this commissioned volume, I have been asked to adopt a helicopter view. This I am happy to do, although I should enter a health warning. I shall not have anything to say about non-certificated adult learning, and not much to say about non-university-based adult learning. Both of these are vital elements in a comprehensive lifelong learning system, and I, like others, rely on NIACE to keep us honest about them. This paper concentrates on the same 'heartland' as a recent report by Nigel Brown and his collaborators entitled *Breaking Out of the Silos: 14–30 Education and Skills Policy* (Brown *et al.* 2004). If we get things right here, the effects should radiate outwards: to build on recent positive developments in pre-school and compulsory education, and to connect with adult lifelong learning and continuous professional development (CPD).

So, what I do want to write about is the problems and prospects of creating an effective system of tertiary education for the UK, which will win more than grudging support from all of the necessary players; in other words a system about which we can feel not only confident, but also proud and affectionate. The seminar agreed that such a horizon-scanning exercise, looking up to ten years ahead, would be a useful contribution.

In getting there, I think that we have three related cultural problems, which are specifically national.

The first is the problem of *reputation*. UK educational life-histories, despite the examples of heroic individuals and groups (in fact, possibly partly because of them) have not been able sufficiently regularly to transcend class determination. What Brown *et al.* call the *royal route* (5+ good GCSEs, 2+ A levels, followed by a full-time degree) dominates patterns of aspiration as well as of analysis (Brown *et al.* 2004, p. 14). Hence Alison Wolf's devastating description of vocational education as being 'a great idea for other people's children' (Wolf 2003, p. 56); hence the battles over fair access to higher education (HE) (and the accusations of *social engineering* – which has become almost as universal an epithet in contemporary British political discourse as *liberal* in the United States); and hence the smug superiority of my first witness:

> *Hardly surprisingly, no deathless prose has been written on 'The Idea of the Tertiary Education Sector'. (Stefan Collini in The London Review of Books, 6 November 2003)*

The second is the problem of *organisation*. British compulsory and post-compulsory education has been through so many waves of *re-organisation* – without sufficient attention to transitions, to legacy arrangements, to unintended consequences, or to sustainability – that we have created a hyper-competitive super-structure (independent and maintained schools, sixth form colleges, and 'academic' faculties in tertiary colleges) and a catch-all sump of a sub-structure (the rest of FE). In fact the Brown report has a more salubrious term: further education is identified there as the *golden thread* (which is chiefly evocative of its precariousness (Brown *et al.* 2004, p. 12)). In the words of my second witness:

> *If the FE sector didn't exist, we would have to invent it. (Kim Howells MP, Minister for Lifelong Learning, Further and Higher Education, Sussex Downs College, 13 October 2004)*

These pathologies converge on the third problem: that of *ambition*. Essentially we have created a fault-line between success and failure post-sixteen because we are scared of the alternative: that of declaring that nobody's publicly supported education and training should cease at 16. In most other advanced economies this is not only unthinkable, it's also illegal. In her 1997 report *Learning Works*, Helena Kennedy was adamant that the threshold level for subsequent happier and more productive lives stands at level 3, not level 2. If we want a high-added-value, knowledge-based, globally competitive economy, we should understand that it is incompatible with maintaining what is called 'the youth labour market'. Here's a third witness, anticipating the Tomlinson proposals:

> *Leading academics and opposition MPs are worried that reducing the number of central tests for 16-year-olds will mean that those who leave school at that age will not have an externally validated qualification to show to employers. (The Independent on Sunday, 17 October 2004)*

Putting this all together, it is clearer why we've got battles going on:

- about whether we need more plumbers than graduates – or more engineers than media studies students;
- about whether dustmen should pay for the higher education of doctors' daughters;
- between independent school heads and the admissions tutors of 'our top universities';
- about whether we spend public money on primary *or* higher education;

and so on.

At the same time, as everybody who is genuinely concerned knows, we face some huge challenges across the range of lifelong learning:

- the challenge of adult literacy (with Claus Moser's 7 million strong army of dysfunctional adults);

- the challenge of prison and juvenile 'care' populations characterised by low or no skills;
- the challenge of school disaffection (including the gender issue – with the hairpin that now opens inexorably between the achievements of girls and boys from SAT 1 onwards);
- the challenge of unpopular or unsupported vocational education;
- the challenge of failing apprenticeship schemes (in which under half of the 'advanced' entrants succeed and under 40 per cent at 'foundation' level);
- the challenge of an apparently unresponsive university system (which now offers more engineering places than there are candidates applying for them);
- the challenge of HE drop-out which (despite its low levels compared with almost all of our international competitors) leaves those who start and fail well behind those who never start on quality of life indicators;

and so on.

Are these different challenges – they certainly affect different organisational sectors? Or are they all part of the same problem? I would argue the latter.

Under careful analysis most of this problem reverts to polarisation, between the (commendably growing) proportion of society which stays engaged and succeeds, and the increasingly isolated but stubbornly significant minority who fall off, and don't get back on:

- the 50 per cent of the population who don't achieve level-2 qualifications;
- the 20 per cent who leave level 3 with low achievements; and
- the 9 per cent who drop out of education, employment and training altogether somewhere between 14 and 19. According to the Paul Hamlyn National Commission on Education Follow-up Group 'the figure rises to 24 per cent if those in jobs but receiving no education or training are added' (National Commission on Educaton Follow-up Group 2003, p. 11).

The same powerful influence of class continues at level 2. In the UK we know that 90 per cent of students with two or more A levels go on to higher education. We also know that only 45 per cent of those with vocational qualifications at this level proceed. The big trap in the UK at the moment is the illusion that *aiming higher* and *widening participation* are the same thing.

The national and international context

By international standards the UK is doing well at some extremely important aspects of HE (research, retention, the global market, etc.). We are also doing well at lifelong learning (including CPD) for those members of society who remain engaged. We are doing less well in the immediate post-compulsory area, and this is where the fork in the road between the engaged and the disengaged appears to be located. As I have already suggested, this is largely because of where this particular sector starts: at 16 formally, and at about 14 informally, with the increasing evidence of disaffection in schools. What we know is that the 'participation gain' generated by the much-needed form of the 16+ examination system is probably now exhausted (Aston 2003). Figure 13.1 gives the stark comparative picture.

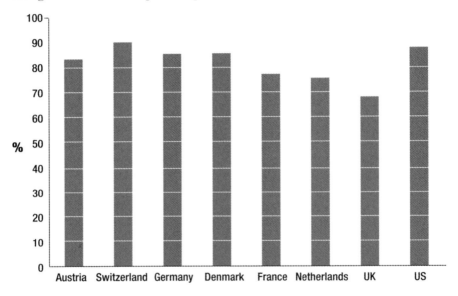

Figure 13.1 Population aged 25–34 with at least upper secondary education (HS graduation) 2001. Source OECD, *Education at a Glance* (2003).

The tertiary event?

Do we now have an opportunity to approach this problem in a systematic and joined-up way? Are we in fact in one of those rare moments of astronomical alignment which could lead to something as dramatic as 'the tertiary event'? The heavenly bodies potentially in alignment include:

- HE via the 2003 White Paper, and the 2004 Act;
- further education (FE) and employers via the Skills Strategy; and
- Schools and related providers via the Tomlinson Report's proposals for 14–19 curriculum and qualification reforms.

You can play all sorts of other interests across this celestial map, including:

- HEFCE, with its plans for lifelong learning networks;
- The Learning and Skills Council (LSC), with its Strategic Area Reviews; and

- The Department for Education and Skills (DfES), with a range of interventions, perhaps not yet quite joined up, like Education Maintenance Allowances (EMA), 'young apprenticeships', and all of the other initiatives in the five-year plan (DfES 2004a).

But let us step back and try to gain a little perspective. Solving this big problem, and the smaller problems which make it up, is going to require attention to both push factors (chiefly about motivation and personal support) and pull factors (chiefly about provision and systems). Would a unified approach to a tertiary system make a positive difference?

Among the things we need to consider at the national level are the levers of positive change, including:

- funding – of learners as well as providers;
- qualification frameworks – credit; 14–19 reform; academic, vocational and mixed forms;
- employment – especially employers' buy-in to training.

But we also have to ask some cultural questions. Educational systems are culturally embedded – what are the implications of wanting to look like, for example:

- Singapore – a society constructed around success in very traditional public examinations;
- or the United States – with its huge Community College network;
- or Australia – with its centrally driven TAFE system;
- or New Zealand – with its universal tertiary entitlement;
- or Germany – where contrary to many people's belief, students now regularly use intermediate-level vocational qualifications to re-enter academic or general higher education?

Here is an 'ambition reality check', about the qualifications and commitment of managers in some of these societies. If this is a measure of capacity at the top of the pyramid, it's worth thinking about the relative expectations each group here has of those who work for them.

Item	UK	USA	Japan	Germany	France
Average terminal education age (1999, years)	19.5	22	21	21	22
Graduate (per cent)	49	74	78	72	61
Days off-the-job training (1998)	4	7	5.5	5.5	6
Days on-the-job training (1998)	4.5	8	6.5	6.5	6

Figure 13.2: Education and Training of British Management. Source: Keep and Westwood 2002, in CIHE 2004.

And here is a 'reputation reality check'. The more successful that national systems are in growing participation and achievement, the greater will be the gap between those who stay on a ladder of educational attainment and those who fall off. We have solid, longitudinal data about the positive effects of participation not only on the economic status of the individual beneficiary (in terms of HE the Government's current almost exclusive selling-point for its reforms), but also on their health and happiness, and on democratic engagement and tolerance; to say nothing of the life chances of their children. I would refer you particularly to the output of the Wider Benefits of Learning Group at the Institute of Education (Bynner *et al.* 2003; Schuller *et al.* 2004). We have a lot of international hand-wringing about 'completion' (or its opposite, 'wastage'). But the big picture is that we don't talk enough about 're-starting' or 're-engagement'.

The most important issue is the growing gulf between a successful majority and a disengaged minority. The illustration in Figure 13.3 is now a little old, but it is one of the most graphic demonstrations of such disengagement. The question that follows is 'Is tertiary education part of the problem, or part of the solution?' The permanently disengaged become the individual self-blamers whose histories have been eloquently mapped by Karen Evans and others (Evans 2003); collectively they make up what Ferdinand Mount calls the newly discovered class of downers (Mount 2004).

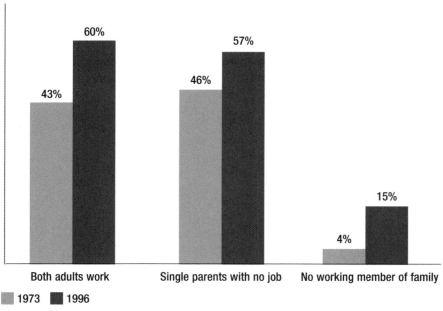

Figure 13.3. Work rich/work poor. Source: Berthoud and Gershuny 2000.

English initiatives

Having talked about *ambition* and *reputation*, let me turn finally to *organisation*, and say a little about the three top current English initiatives. In doing so, I should enter a second health warning. What follows is indeed almost exclusively about England. Things are different in Scotland, Wales and Northern Ireland, not least in terms of legislative and administrative responsibilities. Nor do I simply mean differential enthusiasm for top-up or variable HE fees. Some of what follows reads across the UK: they too have culturally embedded challenges of ambition, organisation and reputation.

A. The case of lifelong learning networks

Here, from an internal HEFCE briefing, is the clearest account I have been able to find of what the Council thinks it is up to with lifelong learning networks (LLNs). It repays careful reading.

LLNs will make a step change in vocational progression in and through HE . . . bring together groups of institutions, including HEIs and FECs, across a city, area or region to offer new progression opportunities for vocational learners. They will:

- combine the strengths of a number of diverse institutions
- provide support for learners on vocational pathways
- bring greater clarity, coherence and certainty to progression opportunities
- develop the curriculum as appropriate to facilitate progression
- value vocational outcomes and provide opportunities for vocational learners to build on earlier learning
- locate the progression strategy within a commitment to lifelong learning, ensuring that learners have access to a range of progression opportunities so that they can move between different kinds of vocational and academic programmes as their interests, needs and abilities develop
- build upon and not duplicate initiatives and activities such as Aimhigher
- include HEIs 'with a research mission as well as those more focused on teaching and learning and engaged in serving local and regional economies'
- offer a guarantee to learners that they will be able to progress from any award offered by one of the partners to any other programme offered within the network that the learner is adequately prepared for, and can benefit from'
- work with SSDA regional partnership managers, SSCs and RDAs
- build on CoVEs, CETLS and Knowledge Exchanges.

Making this commendable 'big idea' work is proving problematic. Some of the problems are conceptual: there's a tension, for example, between *vocational* and *vocational and academic* ambitions for progression. There's the characteristic emphasis on all types of HEIs: 'it won't be worth it without the Russell Group'. But above all, like the Schwartz report on admissions to HE, it founders upon the impossible guarantee: that if we all behave properly, every student will end up where he or she deserves. Supply will match demand as if managed by Adam Smith's invisible hand.

Finally, it remains unclear as to how it will be carried forward. HEFCE are processing applications for LLNs in an overtly competitive manner, through their Strategic Development Fund, and thereby incidentally maintaining the illusion that all relevant activity will be 'within region' (or sub-region). As for the other major partner, the gossip is that the national LSC is backing off any funding commitment, not least as it measures the costs of the new level-2 entitlement (see below).

B. The case of the Skills Strategy

Meanwhile in another part of the forest, a multi-departmental Whitehall initiative is attempting to drive similarly joined-up thinking in terms of work-related skills (DfES/DWP/HMT/DTI 2003).

As Nigel Brown and his team conclude, the Skills White Paper does what government knows it can do best: it sets out measures aimed at 'increasing employer and individual engagement in the publicly-funded system' (Brown et al. 2004, p. 19). Outside this framework it is heavily dependent upon the employer-led Sector Skills Council network, a national Skills Alliance, and regional partnership arrangements. Its principal funding recommendation is, however, unambiguously remedial: a free tuition entitlement for 19–30-year-olds without level-2 qualifications, which colleges are already saying is skewing LSC-channelled funding away from the level-3 qualifications that are necessary to make initiatives like LLNs work.

C. 14–19: the case of the Tomlinson report

Mike Tomlinson's report (DfES 2004b) is universally acknowledged as being very clever. It puts together the full range of 14–19 curriculum and qualifications options and components (including across the academic/vocational divide) into grouped awards at four levels. It includes compulsory elements, although how long ICT can legitimately be isolated from almost every other subject remains a pedagogic question. It breaks the link between ages and stages. It aims simultaneously to reduce the burden of external examination, to restore teacher autonomy, and to allow the best and the brightest to distinguish themselves, not least through the 'extended project' or 'personal challenge'. It is one of the first comprehensive proposals for the system which takes seriously the questions of piloting, of transition and of respect for students part-way through what may be their only, and in most cases their best, chance at the official educational ladder. As a result it proposes a ten-year timetable for full adoption.

Without courageous implementation and without almost universal assent, its very cleverness may contain the seeds of its own destruction. An edifice like this is so inherently complex that it must avoid the reduction (in areas like equivalences and credit accumulation) to an incomprehensible lowest common denominator. And, because it fits together so neatly, it will be destroyed by selective acceptance or cherry-picking.

Conclusion: problems and prospects

In all three cases, we have been there before. Lifelong learning networks were presaged by the 'big partnership', progenitor of the Partnerships for Progression (P4P) initiative which itself issued into the complex and still just about extant framework of Aimhigher. The Sector Skills Development Agency, and its Councils, have their precedents in the Manpower Services Agency, and the full edifice of the National Council for Vocational Qualifications. Sorting out the school curriculum for public examinations at 16 and 18 has literally been a biennial affair since the mid-1970s, as set out in Appendix 3 of the Nuffield Foundation 14–19 Inquiry's first annual report.

How can it be different this time? I'll conclude with two philosophical starters.

First, *who are the stake-holders, really* – who are the people with stakes on the table?

In the good old bad old days, progress in social policy was a simpler affair. Pressure on politicians led them to either invest or not in public services, for which they more or less took responsibility. Mrs Thatcher essentially replaced this uni-directional tendency with a more complex triangle, distancing the politicians from both the services and a new class of 'stakeholders'.

Under these conditions – unambiguously adopted by New Labour – the most common outcome is when government and the stakeholders – two corners – gang up on the public-sector provider as the third. The problem is that the stakeholders are frequently anything but. To take an example, Alison Wolf's *Does Education Matter?* ruthlessly exposes the role of the Confederation for British Industry (CBI) in the great National Vocational Qualifications (NVQ) debacle, culminating in the attempted whitewash of the Beaumont Report:

> *Developed 'for' and supposedly by business, they [NVQs] were consistently neglected by vast numbers of employers both before and after Beaumont. Senior managers were happy to assure government researchers and surveys that they had not only heard of NVQs but were also making them available to their workforce. But the facts spoke otherwise [as they often do in education policy]: by the mid 1990s only 2 per cent of that workforce actually reported themselves to be working towards any sort of NVQ, employer supported or not. (Wolf 2003, pp. 111–16)*

Employers will claim that this is misleading; that most of their training is independent of the publicly funded and validated system – the Brown report estimates up to 89 per cent (Brown *et al.* 2004, p. 18). However, from the employee or learner perspective, this can be small comfort: not much of it is accredited (even to industry standards), and, critically, very little is portable in an increasingly fluid labour market.

Nor is it fair to put all of the blame on employers. There is at least as much which can be laid at the door of partisan politicians, who sweep away their predecessors' partnership structures to replace them with their own brands, forgetting that 'out there' such groups have to be populated by exactly the same people, who have grown weary of successive new dawns. Research, for politicians and their officials, is instant and invariably premature 'evaluation' (Unwin 2004, p. 156). Meanwhile, their volatility (Anthony King once called it being governed by a tribe of hyperactive children) is all too often matched by the inflexibility and professional disdain of the educational establishment. The bottom line is that to be a proper stakeholder you have to put some investment at risk. If you don't, it's all too easy to fulfil the public sector manager's stereotype of a stakeholder as 'someone who can do you harm'.

Secondly, *where is the public interest in all of this?* I would like to suggest one radical new approach. In responding to the 'tertiary moment', all of the potential interest groups have been hair-trigger quick to identify and polemicise hits and misses from their own perspective. What about replacing this unedifying and dysfunctional shouting match with a self-denying ordinance? What would each group be prepared to forego in order to help some of the other groups out of their own dead-ends, or to make better sense of the whole? Implementing the Tomlinson Report would be a good natural experiment for trying this approach.

The educational community is, by its nature, professionally argumentative. From this quality are derived many of its strengths. However, as I argued over a decade ago, it is susceptible to a damaging pathology, the *asymmetrical sympathy syndrome*: every group knows exactly what is going wrong and who else should put it right (Watson 1994, p. 80). For the parties identified above to make the most of the 'tertiary event' we shall have to do better than this. We shall have to come out of our silos (Brown *et al.* 2004). We shall have to get past the deficit model of education and training (Unwin 2004). We shall have to agree on direction of travel, as in Tomlinson's carefully constructed implementation plan (DfES 2004b, Appendix L). We shall have to put more trust in students who have different, and frequently sounder, ideas about what is going to be good and more productive for them than their elders and betters (Wolf 2003, p. 93). And we shall need a newly forged commitment to steadiness and mutual respect if we are to achieve what the current Secretary of State calls 'a system that drives its own improvement more and more' (DfES 2004a, p. 5).

References

Aston, L. (2002) *Higher Education Supply and Demand to 2010*. Oxford: HEPI.

Berthoud, R., J. Gershuny (eds), (2000) *Seven Years in the Lives of British Families: Evidence on the Dynamics of Social Change from the British Household Panel Survey*. Bristol: Policy Press and Institute for Social and Economic Research.

Brown, Nigel, Mark Corney and Geoff Stanton (2004) *Breaking Out of the Silos: 14–30 Education and Skills Policy*. London: Nigel Brown Associates.

Council for Industry and Higher Education (CIHE) (2004) *Solving the Skills Gap: Summary Report from a AIM/CIHE Management Research Forum*. London: CIHE.

Department for Education and Skills (DfES) (2004a) *Five Year Strategy for Children and Learners.* London: The Stationery Office.

Department for Education and Skills (DfES) (2004b) *Final Report of the Working Group on 14–19 Reform.* Nottingham: DfES.

Department for Education and Skills (DfES), Department of Work and Pensions (DWP), HM Treasury (HMT) and Department of Trade and Industry (DTI) (2003) *21st Century Skills: Realising Our Potential – Individuals, Employers, Nation,* Cm. 5810 (July). London: Stationery Office.

Evans, Karen (2003) *Learning for a Living? The Powerful, the Dispossessed, and the Learning Revolution,* University of London Institute of Education professorial lecture, 19 February. London: Institute of Education.

Higher Education Funding Council for England (HEFCE) (2002) *The Wider Benefits of Higher Education: Report by the Institute of Education,* Report 01/46 (July). Bristol: HEFCE.

Mount, Ferdinand (2004) *Mind the Gap: The New Class Divide in Britain.* London: Short Books.

National Commission on Education Follow-up Group (2003) *Learning to Succeed: The Next Decade,* Occasional Paper. Brighton: University of Brighton Education Research Centre.

Nuffield Review of 14–19 Education and Training (2004) *Annual Review, 2003–04.* London: Nuffield Foundation.

Schuller, Tom, John Preston, Cathie Hammond, Angela Brassett-Grundy and John Bynner (2004) *The Benefits of Learning: The Impact of Education on Health, Family Life and Social Capital.* London: Routledge Falmer.

Unwin, Lorna (2004) 'Growing beans with Thoreau: rescuing skills and vocational education from the UK's deficit approach', *Oxford Review of Education* 30.1 (March), pp. 147–60.

Watson, David (1994), 'Living with ambiguity: some dilemmas of academic leadership', in Jean Bocock and David Watson (eds), *Managing the University Curriculum: Making Common Cause.* Buckingham: SRHE and Open University Press, pp. 77–85.

Wolf, Alison (2002) *Does Education Matter? Myths about Education and Economic Growth.* London: Penguin.

Biographies

Prof Robert G. Burgess, Vice-Chancellor, University of Leicester

Professor Robert Burgess is Vice-Chancellor of the University of Leicester. He is a sociologist by training, who has conducted research on schools and higher education. Before joining the University of Leicester in 1999 he was at the University of Warwick, where he was Director of the Centre for Educational Development, Appraisal and Research, Professor of Sociology and Senior Pro-Vice-Chancellor

Dr Philip C. Candy, Director, NHSU Institute, National Health Service University

Professor Philip Candy is the Director of Research and Development, and also Director of the NHSU Institute, within the corporate educational provider for the National Health Services in England (NHSU). He was previously National Research Fellow with the Australian Department of Education, Science and Training, where he examined online and technologically assisted learning across the lifespan. Prior to that he was Deputy Vice-Chancellor (Scholarship) at the University of Ballarat. His 1991 book, *Self-direction for lifelong learning*, published in the United States, won the prestigious Cyril Houle World Award for Literature in Adult Education. He has researched and published widely on Australian higher education and adult learning. He has an enduring interest in the subject of self-directed and lifelong learning in both formal and non-formal contexts. Committed to those institutions, processes and programs that assist people to continue learning throughout their lives he was, as part of the Victorian Learning Towns network (Australia) inaugural Chair of the *'Ballarat: A Learning City'* Advisory Board

Kath Dentith, Assistant Director, Access, Quality Assurance Agency for Higher Education

Kath Dentith joined the Quality Assurance Agency for Higher Education (QAA) in 1998, where she is an Assistant Director. She is responsible for managing and developing the QAA Recognition Scheme for Access to HE and other matters related to QAA's regulation of Access provision, including the production of national data about Access to HE.

Her career background lies principally in further and adult education. She taught first in Leicester, during the 1970s; then in Liverpool, where she first became involved in the delivery and development of Access. In 1994, she moved to a new post in Gloucestershire, where she managed a number of Access programmes, before moving to her current role at QAA.

Prof Chris Duke, Associate Director Higher Education, NIACE and RMIT University

Professor Chris Duke, a historian and sociologist, is Associate Director HE for NIACE, honorary Professor of Lifelong Learning at Leicester, and Professor of Regional Partnership and Learning at RMIT in Melbourne.

He was formerly President of the University of Western Sydney Nepean and has held chairs in lifelong learning there, at Auckland and at Warwick where he was founding Head of the Department of Continuing Education and a Pro-Vice-Chancellor. He has served widely in honorary professional and non-governmental roles internationally, in Australia, the UK and Europe, and writes prolifically on adult non-formal and lifelong learning, higher education, organisational behaviour and the (mis)management of change. He has an abiding interest in education to support sustainable and equitable development

Prof Neil Garrod, Deputy Vice-Chancellor, Thames Valley University

Neil Garrod graduated in Management Sciences at the University of Manchester Institute of Science and Technology and gained his doctorate in operations research at the same institution. He has held academic positions at the University of Wales, at Aberystwyth and Bangor and at the University of Glasgow where he was also Head of the Department of Accounting and Finance and Dean of the Faculty of Law and Financial Studies. He became Executive Dean at the University of the Witwatersrand before returning to Europe as Deputy Vice Chancellor at Thames Valley University.

Laurence Howells, Director of Learning Policy and Strategy, Scottish Funding Council

Laurence Howells is Director of Learning Policy and Strategy at the Scottish Further and Higher Education Funding Councils. His responsibilities include quality assurance and enhancement, teaching and learning policies, strategic development and patterns of provision for both further and higher education in Scotland. He was recently seconded to the Scottish Executive reviewing quality assurance arrangements across the post-16 education sectors.

He graduated in Mathematics at Southampton University and first worked for the British Library in Yorkshire and in London before becoming Assistant Education Officer for the London Borough of Waltham Forest.

Prof Geoff Layer, Pro-Vice-Chancellor, University of Bradford and Director, Action on Access

Geoff Layer is Pro-Vice Chancellor (Learning and Teaching) at the University of Bradford and Professor of Lifelong Learning. He is also the Director of Action on Access, the National Co-ordination team for widening participation in higher education in England. He was the founding Dean of the School of Lifelong Education and Development at Bradford and prior to that Head of Access and Guidance at Sheffield Hallam University.

Prof Sir Howard Newby, Chief Executive, Higher Education Funding Council for England

Sir Howard Newby joined the Higher Education Funding Council for England as Chief Executive in October 2001.

Prior to that he was Vice-Chancellor of the University of Southampton and before that Chairman and Chief Executive of the Economic and Social Research Council, Professor of Sociology at the University of Essex and Professor of Sociology and Rural Sociology at the University of Wisconsin, Madison.

Professor Newby has published widely on social change in rural England and was for eight years a Rural Development Commissioner, responsible for the economic and social regeneration of rural England. He has also been President of Universities UK, and of the British Association for the Advancement of Science. He was awarded a CBE in 1995 for his services to social science and a knighthood in 2000 for his services to higher education.

Prof Gareth Parry, University of Sheffield

Gareth Parry is Professor of Education at the University of Sheffield. He worked in further education colleges and open college networks in London before moving to posts at City, Warwick and Surrey Universities and the Institute of Education, University of London. His current research is concerned with higher education in further education settings. He was a consultant to the Dearing inquiry into higher education in the UK and is Co-Editor of *Higher Education Quarterly*.

Adrian Perry, Senior Visiting Fellow, University of Sheffield

Adrian Perry is a Senior Visiting Fellow at the University of Sheffield, and works as a consultant for clients that include the DfES, LSC, Office of Public Sector Reform, and LSDA, also undertaking pro-bono work with schools and colleges. He was Principal of Lambeth College from 1992 to 2002, having previously been a Principal in Sheffield.

He holds an honorary Doctorate in Education from London South Bank University, and was appointed OBE for services to education in the 2003 New Year Honours. He writes widely on educational policy, with recent articles on fee policy, performance indicators and crisis management.

Prof Richard Taylor, Director, Institute of Continuing Education, University of Cambridge

Richard Taylor is Professor of Continuing Education and Lifelong Learning and Director of the Institute of Continuing Education at the University of Cambridge. Previously he was, Professor of Continuing Education at the University of Leeds, Head of School and Dean of the Faculty of Business, Law, Education and Social Sciences. He is a former secretary of the Universities Association for Continuing Education (UACE) and is currently Chair of the NIACE Policy Committee. He is author or co-author of 12 books, most recently with David Watson *Lifelong Learning and the University: a post-Dearing agenda*; and with Jean Barr and Tom Steele *For a Radical Higher Education: After Postmodernism*.

Prof David Vincent, Pro-Vice-Chancellor, Open University

Professor David Vincent was appointed, in October 2003, to the post of Pro-Vice-Chancellor (Strategy Planning & External Affairs) at The Open University where he holds responsibilities for funding council and governmental liaison, the University's strategic development and its collaborative partnerships.

Prior to this appointment he held a senior management position as Deputy Vice-Chancellor at the University of Keele from 1994 until September 2003, where he had overall charge of the University's academic strategy.

He is a Professor of Social History with an interest in mass communication, secrecy and privacy, and autobiography. He is currently writing on the History of Literacy, and on Secrecy and Privacy in the Modern World 1800-2000.

Prof Sir David Watson, Vice-Chancellor, University of Brighton

Professor Sir David Watson is an historian, and has been Vice-Chancellor of the University of Brighton (formerly Brighton Polytechnic) since 1990. He is also Professor of the History of Ideas. In September 2005 he moves to the Institute of Education, University of London, as Professor of Higher Education Management. Recent books include *Lifelong Learning and the University* (1998), *Managing Strategy* (2000), *New Directions in Professional Higher Education* (2000), *Higher Education and the Lifecourse* (2003), and *Managing Institutional Self-Study* (2005).

He has contributed widely to developments in UK higher education, as a member of Boards and Committees of the Council for National Academic Awards, the CNAA Council and the Polytechnics and Colleges Funding Council, and the Higher Education Funding Council (England). He chaired the HEFCE Quality Assessment Committee and was a member of its Learning and Teaching Committee between 1998 and 2003. He was a member of the Paul Hamlyn Foundation's National Commission on Education of the National Committee of Inquiry into Higher Education chaired by Sir Ron Dearing, and of the Roberts Review of Research Assessment in 2002-03. He was chair of UACE between 1994 and 1998, and currently chairs the Longer Term Strategy Group of Universities UK. He is a Member of the Institute for Learning and Teaching in Higher Education, a Companion of the Institute of Management, and was knighted in 1998 for services to higher education.

Kevin Whitston, Head of Widening Participation, Higher Education Funding Council for England

Kevin Whitston joined the Higher Education Funding Council as Head of Widening Participation at the end of 2003. He was formerly Director of the Widening Participation Unit at the University of Birmingham and prior to that taught for many years in trade union education

Index